'RACE' IN BRITAIN TODAY

RICHARD SKELLINGTON

WITH PAULETTE MORRIS

WITH AN INTRODUCTORY ESSAY BY PAUL GORDON

SAGE PUBLICATIONS

in association with

The Open University

First published 1992

SAGE Publications Ltd
6 Bonhill Street
London EC2A 4PU

SAGE Publications Inc
2455 Teller Road
Newbury Park, California 91320

SAGE Publications India Pvt Ltd
32 M-Block Market
Greater Kailash – I
New Delhi 110 048

British Library cataloguing in publication data

Skellington, Richard
'Race' in Britain Today
I. Title II. Morris, Paulette
305.800941
ISBN 0–8039–8689 0
ISBN 0–8039–8690 4 pbk

Library of Congress catalog card number 92–50116

Designed by the Graphic Design Group of The Open University

Typeset by The Open University

Printed and bound in the United Kingdom by Staples Printers Rochester Limited, The Stanhope Press, Neptune Close, Medway City Estate, Frindsbury, Rochester, Kent

CONTENTS

List of figures, maps and tables

9

FOREWORD

The authors would like to thank the Runnymede Trust, the Commission for Racial Equality, the Child Poverty Action Group and the Radical Statistics Race Group, particularly the authors of *Britain's Black Population* (Bhat *et al.*, 1988) for their valuable assistance. Within the Open University special gratitude is due to Kate Hunter, who edited the book, Lesley Passey, who designed it, Sally Baker, the School of Education liaison librarian who worked so hard obtaining illustrations and original newspaper cuttings and photographs, and to Aileen Lodge, who typed the material and coped heroically with the many changes.

We also want to thank James Donald for the contribution he made to the production of the final draft, June Evison, Sheila Gilks, Chris Golding, June Humphreys, Riz Sharma and Marie-Claude Bovet for their help with previous drafts and artist Alison George and designer Sian Lewis.

INTRODUCTION:
A DIFFERENT REALITY

For the most part ... Britain's well-established black population is still occupying the precarious and unattractive position of the earlier immigrants. We have moved, over a period of eighteen years, from studying the circumstances of immigrants to studying the black population of Britain only to find that we are still looking at the same thing ... There is just the same need now as in 1976 for action to give black people access to widening economic opportunities and life chances; and there is just the same need to pursue equality between racial groups in Britain.

(Brown, 1984, p. 323)

Looking ahead, we should be able to set our work of eliminating racial discrimination in education, housing services and the administration of justice within a firmer context of information and data during the 1990s ... these sources of data will open up opportunities to identify patterns of disadvantage and possible discrimination, and will pinpoint, for the benefit of service providers as will as service customers, the policy, training and resource needs that must be met to overcome any discrimination that is identified.

(Commission for Racial Equality, 1990a, p. 19)

We just want to be ourselves.
We want to do our own thing.
We don't want no discrimination.
That's not a lot to ask for – it's very basic – but we can't get it!

(Black youths quoted in West Midlands County Council, 1986, p. 61)

This book was designed in the first instance to be used by students taking the Open University third level course, ED356 *'Race', Education and Society*. It constructs a profile of minority ethnic groups in the United Kingdom across a wide range of institutional areas – in education, the labour market, the criminal justice system, health, welfare and housing – and places this profile in demographic and historical perspective. The profile is also illustrated in relation to key issues confronting Britain in the 1990s, for example, other inequalities in society, immigration policy, poverty, and racism in Britain. It locates minority ethnic groups and their experiences in relation to the rest of the UK population, and has sought evidence which allows controls to be established across a range of factors: for example, in relation to age, class, gender, and location. A particular emphasis has been placed upon the experiences of young black people, especially with regard to racism, racial harassment, and across the breadth of institutional contexts negotiated in daily life.

Paul Gordon's article, 'The racialization of statistics', examines the ways in which statistics about minority ethnic groups are defined, analysed and interpreted in British society. He shows how the collection of data is not a neutral exercise, but is inevitably conducted from particular ideological perspectives. He also raises fundamental questions about the relationship between data collection and policy implementation, and highlights some of the key implications for minority ethnic groups as knowledge about their 'life chances' and relative status increases.

Part 2 consists of eleven inter-related sections that draw together the results of an extensive survey of existing research and statistical findings. We have included relevant material available up to mid-1991.

The Commission for Racial Equality (CRE) has long argued for the need to monitor and evaluate in order to measure how successfully racism is being combatted. Statistical information can enable organizations to tackle problems that arise in implementing policy strategies, to keep policies under review, and to overcome internal resistance to change. However, some members of minority ethnic groups have expressed doubts and concerns about the need for and the use to which these 'new' statistics will be put. Why are more statistics necessary when there may already be sufficient official and independent research evidence documenting both the extent of racial inequality and the processes which produce it? Why have decades of monitoring and evaluation, however partial, failed to produce effective policy implementation in areas particularly designed to remedy the historic consequences of racial discrimination and disadvantage? These questions raise sensitive issues and complex debates. Robert Moore's evidence to the Home Affairs Committee still rings true: 'statistics have seldom been used to the advantage of the black population, but have been the basis for abuse and for building a climate of opinion in which "the numbers game" proclaims that blacks are intrinsically a problem' (Home Affairs Committee, 1983, p. 138).

We have tried to avoid this 'numbers game' approach to 'race' statistics. In attempting to produce as representative a profile as possible, we have no wish to reify dubiously valid ethnic categories. As Ahmed and Sheldon (1991) have argued, data collection is not an end in itself, and neither should the rising mountains of research into the 'life chances' of black people provide the illusion of progress; evidence is no substitute for action. It must also be recognized that many of the disadvantages described in this profile also apply to white British people. Our focus here, however, is on black British people.

In producing this profile of Britain's black and Asian population, we have been aware of two important issues that arise from our survey of existing research and statistical findings. One is the problem of categorization and terminology; the other is the range and variety of sources used.

There is no one agreed set of terms in use among researchers in this field for the different minority ethnic groups. Sometimes differences in terminology reflect the use of different words for the same or similar groups (such as 'West Indian' and 'Afro-Caribbean'). At other times, different sets of terms refer to different classifications and different ways of classifying. For example, a classification may be based on skin-colour, or country of origin, or descent. Terminology is also problematic because, over time, the terminology itself shifts: some terms fall into disuse and disrepute, while others change. Many terminological uses are controversial, and probably none is without its drawbacks. What was broadly acceptable in the 1980s may not be acceptable in the 1990s, and so on. We have generally adopted the categories used by our sources.

But here we confront a second important issue: the type of data sources used. It is axiomatic that all sources should be treated with degrees of caution. As Gordon's analysis of the 'racialization' of statistics shows, there was in the 1970s and 1980s a relative dearth of consistent minority ethnic group monitoring across many areas of institutional life in Britain. Gordon also emphasizes how the official statistics have changed, and how shifting definitions, for example in the context of our discussion of the labour market in Section 10, have rendered analysis problematic. Sometimes governments have dropped a particular measure altogether, making trend analysis impossible to sustain, for example, in relation to the discussion of poverty in Section 4.

Apart from the work by the Runnymede Trust and the Radical Statistics Race Group (RSRG) in the 1980s, there have been few attempts to produce the kind of profile presented here.[1] In the introduction to the first study of Britain's black population, compiled in the late 1970s, Usha Prashar, then director of the Runnymede Trust, and Dave Drew of the RSRG wrote that in some areas there was a complete 'statistical vacuum' and in others 'a partial vacuum' (Runnymede Trust and RSRG, 1980, pp. xii–xiii). Ten years later, the situation had improved, but the range of sources quoted in this book bears testimony to the need for more monitoring that permits analysis over time by using a smaller range of agreed categories and terminology. We are still at the mercy of our sources.

It is important to recognize, too, that what is presented here is a selection. A diverse range of sources has been used: for example, official government statistics, national and local surveys of circumstances, attitudes and opinions, studies of one ethnic group in more than one locality, comparative research into black and white outcomes, experiential research studies, newspaper and journal articles, policy statements from individuals involved in particular institutional contexts, personal statements from individuals in particular institutional contexts, and statements from individuals reflecting their own experiences – particularly from young black people.

Overall, the trends which emerge from analysis of this data are disturbing. While there is some room for optimism, more pressure from black communities is required to transform political agendas on 'race' issues. Changes will also be needed in legislation. The CRE has argued for tougher laws to challenge entrenched forms of discrimination that still persist after 25 years of race relations legislation (CRE, 1991a). The role and power of organizations such as the CRE may also require radical overhaul and proper funding.

What took place in the 1980s represents, according to Gordon, a deepening of the division in British society along the lines of 'race' and skin-colour. He argues that minority ethnic groups continue to experience *a different reality*:

> Black and white people, as the writer Salman Rushdie remarked some years ago, inhabit different worlds ... It is black people who suffer the degradations, the injustices and the threats to their security of the immigration control system. They who are required to produce their passports to establish their immigration status and the legality of their presence here when they claim benefits or seek services. They who are attacked in their homes, schools and public places because of their physical appearance. They who are regarded by people in authority, and portrayed in the press, as an alien threat from which the rest of society must be defended. This is the reality of racism in Britain in the late 1980s, a reality which contradicts any rhetoric of equality or equal opportunities. (Gordon, 1989a, p. 26)

Young people, and young black people in particular, have become increasingly vulnerable. In June 1991, Michael Day, chair of the CRE, observed:

> We have come a long way since 1966 but there are still too many token gestures. The achievements of many from the minority ethnic communities are impressive, but young black people in particular do not feel valued. Many of the social factors which contributed to inner city disturbances of 10 years ago are still apparent.
>
> (*Independent*, 15 June 1991)

Will the 1990s see these 'token gestures' transformed into effective policies? Will the 'social factors' underlying the profile presented here be radically changed?

Richard Skellington
Paulette Morris
October 1991

Notes

1   The Runnymede Trust and the Radical Statistics Race Group (1980); Bhat *et al.* (1988). The Runnymede Trust publish *Race and Immigration*, a monthly bulletin which is a valuable source for updating much of the material presented here. (See list of useful addresses at the back of this book.)

PART 1

THE RACIALIZATION OF STATISTICS

Paul Gordon

A personal prologue

A few weeks before beginning to write this section, I received a telephone call at the Runnymede Trust, the small education, research and information body concerned with problems of racism and discrimination. The caller was a television journalist who was thinking about making a short film on racial attacks in East London. She was unclear about what the Runnymede Trust actually was but had heard from a colleague that we 'collected statistics' and wanted to know what statistics we had on racial violence in the London Borough of Tower Hamlets. I explained that, while we did indeed have much statistical information, this was only a small part of the material we held in our library and files. As for racial attacks, I went on to explain, we probably did have some figures but there were a number of serious problems with these. First, the only ones available were those collated by the Metropolitan Police and it was widely accepted, both by the police and by those campaigning on the issue, that they represented but a small fraction of all incidents; the vast majority, perhaps as much as 90 per cent, were not reported to the police. Secondly, there was the problem of definition. The concept of racial attacks, as it is most commonly understood, refers to attacks which are in some way racially motivated (which does not rule out other motives). In the context of Britain, this means overwhelmingly attacks by whites on blacks since few attacks on whites by blacks could be said, in any meaningful sense, to be motivated by racism. The definition used by the police, on the other hand, refers to 'inter-racial incidents'; that is, incidents in which aggressor and victim come from different ethnic groups and which could, and did, include attacks by blacks on whites. Thirdly, there were problems in interpreting statistics such as these since increases or decreases were as likely to reflect tendencies to report incidents as they were to reflect the actual prevalence of the problem.

I could sense a growing impatience, possibly irritation, on the part of the caller. After all, I seemed to be standing in the way of some information that she wanted. So, she asked, how was one, how were they, to measure any rise or fall in racial attacks in the area? I suggested that they might talk to people in the area, local residents and workers, for instance, or to community organizations, the police, and so on. That way they might get a better picture of what was happening. To the journalist, however, this would not provide *facts*, only impressions, opinions. What she needed was facts and these could only come in statistical form.

I offer this story because it provides an example, typical in my experience, of the way in which many people look at statistical information. Here was someone committed to an idea of journalistic objectivity, looking for objective factual information and seeing in statistical data the most factual and objective kind of information available. The lived experience of human beings, while undoubtedly interesting was, as far as this journalist was concerned, simply not factual enough. In effect, she was defining reality in terms of what could be measured. This, of course, is not something that is peculiar to journalists. We all, at some point or another, want some kind of factual information to support cases we are making, arguments we are putting forward, and to many people there is nothing as factual and objective – and incontrovertible – as a statistic.

Until the mid-1980s relatively little statistical information on black people in Britain was collated at a national level or in any systematic way. The three main categories of such information were: those of the national population census held every ten years, which had asked in 1971 and 1981 a question about the country of birth of heads of households; the Labour Force Survey (LFS) carried out every two years on people in the workforce; and the statistical data collected on a continuing basis in connection with immigration control, such as the number of people accepted for settlement or making short-term visits. There were virtually no data collected nationally and regularly in the fields of education, health, welfare, social services, the criminal justice system, policing, racial violence, or housing. It was thus impossible to know, for instance, how many black pupils there were in schools or education authority areas; how many black teachers and at what grades; the number and seniority of black doctors and nurses; the extent of racial violence; or the proportion of black people going through the criminal courts. This presented considerable problems for both academics and policy-makers who could obtain such information only through specific research projects and, sometimes, through locally-based surveys.

At the time of writing, data are collected or are planned to be collected on a considerably expanded range of areas including the ethnic origins of school pupils and school teachers, students in higher and further education, people on probation, the prison population, and on racial incidents (using the police's definition mentioned above). In addition, and of great importance both symbolically and practically, the census in 1991 was the first to ask a question about the ethnic origins of respondents. This expanded data collection reflects the conversion of policy-makers and administrators at various levels to the cause of equal opportunities.

What accounts for these changes? How are we to understand what seems to be a greater acceptability of racial monitoring of one kind or another? Why is information being collected on some aspects and not on others? To what uses will this information be put? These are some of the questions that I shall try to answer. At the same time, I want to look critically at the statistics that are collected on black people, in the same way that I tried to do with the journalist, although in more detail and by looking at a number of different areas. By looking at the way in which statistics are defined and analysed and the decisions which lie behind whether or not to collect information, I hope to illustrate some of the problems of official data on matters related to race. A case history of the development of ethnic statistics in education helps me to suggest some answers to the questions just posed in relation to that field of policy.

The construction of racial data

When thinking about ethnic or racial data it is important to keep in mind that such data are not just a reflection of objective reality which is 'out there', as it were, and that simply has to be recorded, counted or measured. Such data have been *racialized*, that is, 'race' has been introduced as a factor of some importance and the subjects defined, at least partly, in racial terms. Thus, for instance, people in a particular group being measured, say, in schools, are not just seen as men, women and children but as men, women and children who belong to particular racial, ethnic, linguistic or religious groups. Such an approach to data depends on a decision being taken that these are, or at least may be, factors of importance in explaining perform-ance or status (as opposed, say, to whether people have short or long hair or wear spectacles which may, of course, be considered important by others in a different context). The use of racial categories, implying racial difference, in other words, implies the existence of some degree of inequality that is based on racial or ethnic difference and that can be quantified.

The collection of racialized data involves a further decision – about the categories to be used. Particularly as the collection of such data becomes more common, it is easy to lose sight of the fact that the categories used are terms that have to be decided. As is pointed out in the introduction to this course, although we talk of 'race' and 'race relations', often without thinking, 'races' – racial categories or racial groups – do not exist as objective biological facts in any meaningful way. The study of human beings has been unable to identify significant characteristics that can be found in some groups of people but not in others that would allow us to define and delineate distinct racial groups. Nor has such study found any differences of ability or intelligence. The differences that do exist between peoples from different parts of the world, particularly the physical characteristics of skin pigmen-tation, bone structure, hair type and so on, are, in themselves, of no importance. Physical characteristics become important only when values are attached to different physical types and when physical differences are seen as outward signs of other character traits or personality types. But these are always *ascribed* by one group to others. For example, Jews may be seen as devious, clannish and mean; Afro-Caribbeans as lazy, disorderly and prone to criminal activity; Asians as dishonest; Latins as volatile and emotional; Scots as mean and dour; Germans as humourless and efficient; English as formal and averse to washing too much; and so on.

'Race', racial groups and categories, in other words, are not things that are given – objective facts waiting to be used – but concepts that have to be *constructed*. This construction involves a number of stages: differences of a certain kind between people have to be discerned; these differences have to be considered consequential; and these perceived shared attributes, such as skin colour, nationality, or regional or ethnic origins, have to become the basis for defining groups or categories of people. This has considerable importance for the collection of racialized data, which can use a wide range of categories as shown in the following examples of the major surveys which involve differentiation along ethnic lines:

1   From 1990, schools are required to collect data on the ethnic origins of pupils and teachers, as well as on their religious and linguistic backgrounds. (This is dealt with in more detail in the case-study of education statistics given later.) The categories used are the same as those developed for the 1991 census (see 3 below).

2   The 1971 census asked respondents about the birthplaces of their parents. The size of the black population was calculated by subtracting the estimated number of people born in the New Commonwealth (all Commonwealth countries except for Australia, Canada and New Zealand), but of non-New Commonwealth, origin from the total number of British residents of New Commonwealth origin, plus those with at least one New Commonwealth-born parent.

3   The 1991 census asked people to select one of nine categories – white, black-Caribbean, black-African, black-other, Indian, Pakistani, Bangladeshi, Chinese, or other.

4   The Labour Force Survey, which looks extensively at patterns of employment and unemployment, uses yet another classification scheme, currently asking respondents if they are white, West Indian or Guyanese, Indian, Pakistani, Bangladeshi, Chinese, African, Arabian, mixed, or other.

5   From 1970–82 the Department of Employment monitored what it referred to as 'coloured' unemployment using the categories of East Africa, other African countries, West Indies, India, Pakistan, Bangladesh (after 1973) and other Commonwealth countries. This monitoring was carried out by staff who identified those considered 'coloured' who were then asked about their country of birth. This scheme was abandoned in 1982 when the responsibility for producing unemployment statistics moved from job centres to unemployment benefit offices. Plans to introduce a new method of monitoring by visual assessment by staff were blocked by unemployment benefit staff. The new scheme would have used three categories – Afro-Caribbean, Asian, others.

6   The General Household Survey, a survey of various social policy issues such as health, marriage and leisure, has since 1983 asked a question on ethnic origin in addition to the questions previously asked on country of birth. The categories used are those used in the LFS.

7   The Metropolitan Police has used its own 'identity code' since 1975 involving six classes: IC1 – white-skinned European types – English, Scottish, Welsh, Scandinavian and Russian; IC2 – dark-skinned

European types – Sardinian, Spanish, Italian; IC3 – Negroid types – Caribbean, West Indian, African, Nigerian; IC4 – Indians and Pakistanis; IC5 – Chinese, Japanese, Mongolians, Siamese; IC6 – Arabians, Egyptians, Algerians, Moroccans and North Africans.

8   The British Crime Survey, which investigates actual as distinct from reported crime and victimization patterns, seeks information on ethnic origins of respondents and, where known, alleged perpetrators of crimes. Categories used are white, black (West Indian or African), Indian, Pakistani or Bangladeshi, and other. (For respondents the last are replaced by 'other non-white' and 'mixed or uncertain'.)

9   Since 1988 all police forces have been required to record details of 'racial incidents' and submit these for central collation.

10 The Prison Department's ethnic monitoring of the prison population uses the same categories as the LFS and is based on self-assessment by prisoners.

11 The Hospital In-Patient Enquiry, completed for all admitted patients, has requested information on the place of birth of patients since 1969, as has the Mental Health Enquiry since 1970.

These examples show that the ethnic or racial categories used in a census or survey are not just there – if they were, the same division would be used all the time – but have to be decided upon and have to be constructed. This is not as simple or as straightforward as it may seem. The only truly objective category in this respect is that of legal nationality. The fact that someone is British, Pakistani, Canadian or Jamaican is a fact of law and verifiable according to established procedures. It is, of course, something quite different from other categories, racial or ethnic, and may not be considered the most important. Thus someone may not wish to be identified in terms of where they were born but in some other way. A Pakistani woman, for example, may think of herself primarily as black or Asian or Muslim. A British-born black girl may think of herself as West Indian or black or British or Afro-Caribbean.

The problems of devising suitable categories, other than legal nationalities, have been discussed by several academics in relation to the question of whether information on ethnicity should be sought in the census. Several academics have drawn attention to the problems involved. Dr Roger Ballard, for example, has said that it is 'virtually impossible to pose askable or answerable questions about "race"' (Home Affairs Committee, 1983), while another writer has stated that 'the search for "races"… has been shown to be a fool's errand' (White, 1979). Frequently, the categories used in a survey are a mixture of racial, national and ethnic classifications. To take the categories for the 1991 census as an example, white and black are pseudo-racial categories, referring, rather inaccurately, to perceived skin colours, but Indian, Pakistani and Bangladeshi are all legal nationalities although they may also be regarded as ethnic categories. Chinese is a nationality, but also an ethnic description as well as a linguistic group, and so on. A further complication arises in that people do not have fixed views of themselves. In the United States only 65 per cent of the population categorized themselves by the same racial or ethnic description from a fixed inventory as they had done the previous year, showing that racial or ethnic identities are not simple or straightforward (Leech, 1989).

Rather than ask about ethnic origins, critics have suggested, a question should be asked directly about colour, although here again problems arise. The description 'black' might be used by some people of Afro-Caribbean origin but not by others, or by some people of Asian origin but not by others, and so on. Similarly, 'white' can include people who are quite different not only in actual skin colour but also in national or ethnic origins, from fair-skinned north Canadians to darker skinned Slavs or people from Mediter-ranean countries. And when skin colour is used, how are people such as Chinese, Japanese, native Americans and Arabs to be designated? (We might note here, too, that the catch-all concept 'non-white' is equally unsatisfactory since it defines its subjects in terms of something else, what they are *not*; that is, white.)

The various censuses and surveys described above also illustrate matters which, by their absence, are not considered sufficiently important to be subject to some kind of racialized data collection. Thus there is no racialized data collection on the numbers of people claiming welfare benefits, using some form of personal social services, seeking health care (other than as in-patients), coming into contact with the police or appearing in court. These gaps are important because they mean that basic information about impor-tant issues is lacking. It is impossible, therefore, for academic researchers and others to make any meaningful comparisons between the experiences of people of different ethnic origins and point to any desirable policy changes.

Even where something is regarded as worthy of being recorded, it may be defined in a way that is problematic. Many people, for instance, argued for a long time that there should be central monitoring by the Home Office of the extent and nature of racial attacks. This is now being done, but the definition used is not that of attacks on people because of their colour or ethnic origin, that is attacks motivated at least in part by racism, but of 'racial incidents' in which victim and assailant are of different ethnic groups and where a racial motive is either suggested by the victim or inferred by a police officer. This means that attacks on white people where the offender is alleged to be black can be and are recorded as 'racial incidents' even if these are, in reality, purely criminal acts and there is no evidence of racial hostility but simply an allegation by the victim or the officer to whom it is reported. The specifically *racist* nature of many white attacks on black people is therefore denied and racial violence is redefined as just another aspect of inter-racial crime.

A final problem to be considered here is the isolation of race or ethnicity from other factors. Obviously, any human being or group of human beings is not defined by any one characteristic. We are not just, for example, men or women. We are men and women who are also of particular age groups, in different parts of the country, with different educational backgrounds, of different ethnic origins, different family responsibilities, with different physical abilities and much more. Any one of these may be important in itself in explaining our position in the job market, for example, or educational achievement, but a more accurate explanation is likely to flow from a cross-fertilization of factors. In many cases where data have been racialized, gender difference is also monitored and account may also be taken of age. So, for instance, if we look at the statistics produced by the Prison Department of the Home Office we can see that, while Afro-Caribbean men are disproportionately represented in the prison population, Afro-Caribbean women are even more disproportionately represented. Here gender and ethnicity appear to interact, suggesting that for an explanation of the numbers of black female prisoners we must look not just at 'race' or ethnicity but also at gender.

There is, however, a major gap in every case of racialized data and that is the absence of any consideration of social class, even though this has been shown in many cases to be a prime explanatory factor for comparative success (or failure). One example of this is that the high achievement of some school pupils of Asian origin compared with their counterparts can be explained to some extent by their social class position. To put it crudely, children from middle-class families on the whole do better in school than those from working-class families. Similarly, the British Crime Survey found relatively high criminal victimization rates among Afro-Caribbeans and Asians but said that this could be explained by the related factors of geographical location and social class. In other words, Asians and Afro-Caribbeans were more likely to be victims of certain crimes than whites not because of their colour but because they were more likely than whites to live in areas of high crime. It is important to bear this in mind, as an emphasis on the single factor of race or ethnicity can lead to social class – or indeed other factors – being ignored and wrong conclusions being drawn.

The collection of racial or ethnic statistics is not then a neutral exercise involving the simple collection of objective facts. Rather, from the start, it involves decisions of a political nature about what to record, in what terms and in what way, stemming from a particular ideological position. To illustrate this more concretely, let us look at two examples of racial statistics; the government statistics on the control of immigration and the more specific example of the crime statistics released by the Metropolitan Police in 1982.

Immigration statistics

Until the mid-1980s, immigration statistics were one of the three main categories of racialized statistics collected in the UK on a systematic basis. Indeed, immigration statistics have been collected for longer than any other category of racial data, since the first restrictions were placed on the immigration of Commonwealth citizens in the Commonwealth Immigrants Act 1962. These statistics, collated by the Home Office, are published annually and provide extensive information on, for example, the numbers and countries of origin of people admitted to the United Kingdom (and the purpose of their visits); those refused admission; people accepted for settlement; and applications for entry clearance from the Indian subcontinent. They also provide some information on the number of people deported each year or removed as alleged illegal entrants.

Why is this information considered sufficiently important that it should be collated and published each year? It may be answered that governments need to know how many people enter and leave the country each year so that they can plan for significant increases or decreases in population and allocate resources to assist the settlement of new immigrants. This is a plausible answer, but it does not hold in this case. The immigration statistics do not record those who left the country. (This is done on a completely different basis, the International Passenger Survey, which uses a different system of definition and categories which makes it impossible to compare its findings with the immigration figures.) Therefore, the purpose of these figures is not to determine loss or gain of population through migration, nor is it to assist the allocation of resources for new immigrants since the figures are concerned only with where people have come from, not where they may be settling. They are thus useless in ascertaining areas of the country where particular social or educational needs might arise.

The answer to why the immigration statistics are collected would appear to have more to do with the commitment of successive governments since the 1960s to policies of strict controls on immigration from the Commonwealth and on the immigration of black people; the annual immigration statistics are evidence of how such policies are working. Thus government statements will frequently point to the decline in the numbers accepted for settlement as proof of the government's fulfilment of its manifesto commitments or to a rise in deportations as evidence both of more effective 'after-entry' controls and of the greater extent of law-breaking. In other words, the statistics seem to be there to appease anti-immigration sentiments. This is not to say that the immigration statistics do not have other uses. Critics of British immigration policies can and do use them to argue that government policies are becoming increasingly harsh, that they have a disproportionate impact on black people, and so on. But their main purpose, it would appear, is to support the government of the day in indicating the effectiveness of government policy.

Crime statistics

My second example is of a particular set of data produced in a particular year, rather than, as with the immigration statistics, continuously over a period of years. In March 1982, the Metropolitan Police issued its statistics on crimes recorded in London in 1981. The figures highlighted two things. First, an 8 per cent rise in serious crime over the previous year and secondly, an increase in 'mugging' and the alleged disproportionate involvement of black people in this crime. The figures stated that the 'appearance of the assailant' had been described as white by just under 5,000 victims, but as 'coloured' by more than 10,000. This was the first occasion on which police statistics had been racialized in this way.

What was the point of collating and then publishing such information? Was this a disinterested exercise on the part of the police? If it had been, would we not have expected the statistics to have presented details of the racial or ethnic origins of alleged victims and offenders in relation to all categories of crime? As it was, the category of 'robbery and other violent theft' was the only category to be racialized in this way. We might also have expected the police statistics to have highlighted other interesting features, for example that the number of homicides had fallen by 36 per cent on the previous year, that assaults had scarcely increased, and that the clear-up rate for reported serious crime had fallen to only 17 per cent. When asked why the police had highlighted this category of offence and done so in this way, Metropolitan Police Deputy Assistant Commissioner Gilbert Kelland said that it had been done in response to 'public opinion and pressure'. When asked how such public opinion was ascertained, he said it was done through the media. A closer analysis reveals, however, that the media, especially sections of the popular press, were not so much reflecting public opinion as constructing it and that this was done partly through the use of statistics leaked by the police. This shows that in the construction of policy agendas, statistics are a powerful tool indeed, precisely because people regard them as indisputable 'facts'. Against the police claim that they were only responding to public opinion, it has been argued that in choosing to link 'race' and crime in the way they did and then highlighting this, the Metropolitan Police were seeking to establish a firm correlation between black people, especially young black men, and street crime. If this were so, one interpretation could be that the police were seeking public support for the introduction of a tactical offensive in areas of significant black settlement. In particular, it has been argued that the police hoped to deflect the criticisms of their operations and methods made by Lord Scarman in his report, published only a few months before, on the Brixton disorders. In other words, it is arguable that the police had *chosen* to racialize these statistics and had done so for their own political reasons. (For more detailed accounts of this episode see Bentley, 1982 and Sim, 1982.)

Arguments for racial data

Political purposes are only one of several reasons why racialized data may be collected. They can be grouped very broadly into three types: simple 'fact-finding'; to inform government policy; and to bring about social reform. These can, of course, overlap, but the distinctions may be useful for descriptive purposes.

Fact-finding

The explanation of 'simple fact-finding' can be used to account for much of the racialized data collection that has existed until now. In this respect, the data is not collected with any apparent aim in mind and once collated is not used for any obvious purpose. This would be true, for example, of the data from the 1971 and 1981 censuses and the Hospital Enquiries mentioned earlier. Here, information was collected on the country of birth of respondents (and in the case of the hospital surveys continues to be collected) without any obvious purpose. It was also true of the data collection on 'immigrant' school pupils between 1966 and 1973 when the then Education Minister, Margaret Thatcher, admitted that no use was made of the data. (This is dealt with in more detail below.) Such information *may*, of course, be used at some point in the future, either by the government department that collects it or by someone else, but this is almost incidental. The main reason for its collection in the first place would appear to be a tendency in bureaucratic societies to gather information for its own sake, but this nevertheless shows the salience of 'race' as an administrative concern, particularly since the racialization of public debate since the 1960s.

Informing government policy

It is more common, of course, for information to be gathered for the reason that it will somehow assist in the exercise of some government policies. The most important example of this in Britain lies in the provision of funding under Section 11 of the Local Government Act 1966. Section 11 allows local authorities with substantial minority ethnic group populations to apply to central government for funding to meet the 'special needs' of such populations. If such applications are successful, central government contributes 75 per cent of the funding. (Originally, local authorities qualified if more than 2 per cent of the school population had parents who were born in the New Commonwealth and Pakistan (NCWP) and who had arrived in the UK in the previous ten years. In 1982, the 2 per cent and ten year criteria were abolished.) Data from the 1981 census is currently used to estimate the numbers and proportion of minority ethnic group populations in particular local authority areas, although this is less important than hitherto as the Home Office, which is responsible for the administration of Section 11 funding, has expanded discretion to fund even authorities with relatively small minority populations. Similarly, the size of local minority ethnic group populations is one of the criteria used by central government in determining the level of support grant to local authorities and in allocating expenditure for alleviating urban poverty and promoting regeneration under the Urban Programme.

Although racialized data is used for these purposes, it should be borne in mind that expenditure under these three headings is comparatively limited. In addition, minority ethnic groups do not necessarily benefit directly from it. Even Section 11 funding, which is supposed to be aimed specifically at meeting the needs of minority populations, has been widely abused by some local authorities who have used such funding for general spending. One result of this was an extensive review by the Home Office of the whole Section 11 spending.

Social reform

The third argument put forward for the collection of racialized data is that it is necessary for the purposes of social reform; that is, that such information is necessary to identify areas where minority ethnic groups may be subject to discrimination and to assist in the implementation of policies aimed at ensuring equal opportunities. Organizations such as the Commission for Racial Equality (CRE) and the Runnymede Trust have argued that without such data it is impossible to identify and locate discriminatory practices, while equal opportunities will remain no more than paper policies and good intentions. In the 1970s, the Runnymede Trust, for example, used census and other data in two influential but very different studies which pointed to systematic discrimination against black people. In 1975, the Trust used information from the 1971 census on the size of the 'coloured' population along with information from the Greater London Council's (GLC) housing department to show that the department's allocation procedures were discriminating against black families (Runnymede Trust, 1975). This led to an investigation by the GLC itself and a revision of allocation procedures (Parker and Dugmore, 1976). Similarly, the Runnymede Trust used census data and statistics gathered by the Metropolitan Police to show that young black men were disproportionately at risk of being arrested and prosecuted under the Vagrancy Act 1824, often known as the 'sus' law, which made it an offence to be a 'suspected person' loitering with the intent to commit a criminal offence, a charge which could be substantiated on the evidence of two police officers and which, many contested, was used by the police in some areas as a means of controlling the movements of young black people. This study played some part in the successful campaign to have the law repealed (Demuth, 1978).

Not only can racialized data be useful in proving discrimination, but the collection of racial statistics is effectively required by law. Since 1968, it has been unlawful to discriminate against someone on racial grounds in employment and housing. Thus, in either field, it is unlawful to give a white person (or a black person for that matter) preferential treatment because of the colour of their skin. This is what the law calls direct discrimination. Since 1976, the law has also prohibited indirect discrimination; that is, practices or procedures that may not be discriminatory themselves but that have the effect of discriminating against a particular racial or ethnic group. An example would be a requirement that workers be of a minimum height, which could not be met by, say, most Bengalis or Chinese, and which could not be justified by the nature of the job in question.

The concept of indirect discrimination would be quite unworkable in the absence of racially-based data about local and national populations, as well as particular workforces. By extension, such data is also essential to the work of the CRE which is charged with implementing the Race Relations Act 1976 and which carries out formal investigations of institutions and organizations to identify possible discriminatory procedures. In the absence of accurate data about the ethnic composition of a local workforce, for example, it would be impossible for the Commission to argue that a workplace where only 2 per cent of staff were black was in fact discriminating in some way. (This, of course, is only part of the story as the Commission has to identify mechanisms that might be excluding workers from a particular group, but it is an essential part.) So, too, the Commission has argued that ethnic monitoring is essential if local authorities are to discharge their responsibilities under Section 71 of the Race Relations Act 1976 to eliminate unlawful racial discrimination and to promote equality of opportunity in all their functions.

Such arguments for collecting racialized data were given considerable impetus in the early 1980s when they were supported by Lord Scarman in his report on the Brixton disorders of 1981 (Scarman, 1981) and the Parliamentary Home Affairs Committee in its wide-ranging enquiry and report on 'racial disadvantage' (Home Affairs Committee, 1981). Both were concerned at the continuing extent of what they saw as racial 'disadvantage', which as the 1980 and 1981 urban disorders showed, and as Lord Scarman had accepted, had been at least contributory factors to the most serious public disorder seen in Britain for a long time. The Home Affairs Committee strongly supported the idea of an ethnic question in the census, complaining that:

it is impossible to discover the simple factual truth about some of the most significant and apparently straightforward matters ... As matters stand we know neither the total ethnic minority population nor their true rate of unemployment ... Inspired guesswork and extrapolation from old and often unreliable national figures is reflected on a local scale.

(Home Affairs Committee, 1981, pp. viii–ix)

The Committee also called for ethnic monitoring by local authorities, employers and others and recommended the production of national figures on the performance of what it called 'West Indian' children.

Arguments against collecting racial data

Many others, however, have questioned the value of ethnic or racial data, often focusing on the issue of the ethnic question in the census. (This section draws on Leech, 1989 and Booth, 1988.)

The political context

First, critics of racial data have questioned the political context in which such information is gathered and the uses to which it might be put. Many people have drawn attention to the context of racially discriminatory immigration controls, the successive withdrawal of rights from Commonwealth citizens (including an automatic right to British citizenship and to be joined in Britain by their families), and the fears of many black people about their status in the UK. Thus Professor Robert Moore, a sociologist who has done a great deal to reveal the existence and operation of racism in Britain, has argued that there has never been a real programme aimed at racial equality in Britain which might support the inclusion in the census of an ethnic question. He has said that while, as a social scientist, he has found the absence of certain data from the census a nuisance, 'given the record of governments since 1961, I would nonetheless advise the black population not to collaborate in the provision of such data in the present circumstances' (Home Affairs Committee, 1983, p. 139). Similarly, another prominent academic in race relations, Professor John Rex, has questioned the value of racial data:

> The benefit which immigrants have had from statistics has been confined largely to help on technical matters, like language instruction. Otherwise, the presence of immigrants has been used as an index of pathology, justifying increased payments to particular local authorities who have all too often used such increased payments for the benefit of their native British citizens.

(*The Times*, 28 January 1980)

Such criticisms reflect the attitude of many black people who have pointed to the extensive research, including statistical analyses, which has been carried out in a number of areas but which has resulted in little by way of action to improve the material lives of the people researched and counted.

It is also argued that racial statistics have invariably been used, not in the interests of black people but, as with immigration figures and police statistics on crime, against them.

Abuse of statistics

Secondly, some critics have claimed that information gathered for one purpose, the census, might be used for other, less acceptable purposes. In the 1970s, for example, many people referred to fears of repatriation or expulsion as one of their reasons for opposition to an ethnic question in the census, or to other forms of ethnic data collection, and pointed to the fact that one firm supporter of an ethnic question in the census was the fascist National Front which advocated a policy of expulsion of all 'non-white' people from Britain. (The Front's support for an ethnic question illustrates how different people can support the collection of data for very different reasons.) While such fears were real, a programme of forced expulsion would not require census data if it were based on the obvious physical attribute of skin colour, although census data would certainly facilitate the planning of such a programme. In this respect, it is also worth noting that discrimination against people on racial grounds is easy without statistics, as the CRE found when it investigated the allocation of housing by the London Borough of Hackney. At the time there was no ethnic record-keeping but the ethnic origins of tenants was relatively easy to ascertain, for instance, through their names or other references (CRE, 1984a).

Problems of definition

Finally, critics have pointed to the difficulties in formulating suitable questions in collecting racialized data, a point looked at earlier in the discussion of how racialized data is constructed. Some have argued that it is impossible to devise a meaningful set of categories and have pointed to the problems arising from existing definitions – that people may define themselves in different ways at different times and in different contexts, and that some categories may mean different things to different people. For example, Chinese is a language as well as a legal nationality but it may also be regarded as an ethnic category.

Although there is now widespread support for various forms of ethnic monitoring and an ethnic question in the census, it should be remembered that critics of such data collection have had some impact. The ethnic question that was to be included in the 1981 census, for example, was dropped after just over half the households in a 1979 test census in the London Borough of Haringey returned their forms. Similarly, in 1980 the Rampton Committee on the education of minority ethnic group children was forced to abandon plans for research into the reasons for under-achievement among West Indian children when it became clear that there was considerable disquiet among black parents about such research, which they felt would stigmatize them. And in 1983, opposition from community organizations prevented research into patterns of crime in the London boroughs of Hackney and Camden. In both cases it was argued that the research was wrongly focused and misguided and would result in the blaming of black people rather than produce any gains for them.

Education and racial statistics: a case study

In 1966 the Department of Education and Science (DES) began to collect statistics on the numbers of 'immigrant' pupils in schools in England and Wales. An immigrant, for the purposes of these statistics, was someone who had been born outside the UK or who was born in the UK to parents who had been in the UK less than ten years. (As was later to be noted by the Swann Committee in its report *Education for All* (DES, 1985), this definition implied that after ten years an immigrant family would cease to suffer from any educational difficulties that could be attributed to immigration and racial difference.)

There were two main reasons for the collection of these statistics. The first was to assist central and local government in making provision for the teaching of English to those whose first language was not English. As a 1965 DES circular put it: 'From the beginning the major educational task is the teaching of English' (DES, 1965). The same year that the collection of 'immigrant' statistics began, provision was made, through Section 11 of the Local Government Act 1966, for local authorities with substantial minority populations to apply to central government for funding to help with special provision.

The second reason for the collection of the statistics had to do with the policies of dispersal of black children advocated by central government and pursued by some local education authorities. In 1963, the then Minister of Education, Edward Boyle, said in Parliament that, where possible, it was 'desirable on education grounds' that no one school should have more than about 30 per cent of immigrants (*Hansard*, 1963). In promulgating what became known as 'Boyle's law', the Minister was responding to a row in Southall, West London, where a group of white parents had protested against the large number of black children at a particular school. This was now, Boyle said, 'irretrievably an immigrant school'. The important thing, he said, 'is to prevent this happening elsewhere'. The policy of dispersal was confirmed by DES Circular 7/65 (ibid.) which said that the chances of assimilating 'immigrant children' became more remote as their numbers increased and that 'serious strains' arose when the proportion went over one-third in a school or class. Catchment areas of schools should be drawn to avoid such concentrations and, where this was impracticable, physical dispersal should be arranged. It is not hard to see that this policy confirmed for many white parents what they already believed – that black pupils *per se* were a problem in schools and a barrier to progress in education. The collection of ethnic data was therefore contributing to the definition of black people as a problem. (The question of dispersal and all-black or all-white schools has, of course, arisen more recently as some white parents have complained about sending their children to schools where the majority of pupils are of Asian or Afro-Caribbean origin and where parental choice of schools has raised the prospect of this development – described by some as educational apartheid – continuing.)

Within a few years, however, the definition used in the statistics was criticized as unsatisfactory by the House of Commons Select Committee on Race Relations and Immigration. The Select Committee said that the statistics gave only an 'indirect indication' of colour and recommended the keeping of statistics on the numbers of 'coloured people' (Select Committee on Race Relations and Immigration, 1969). As a result of the Committee's report, the DES undertook to revise its definition. In 1973, however, the Select Committee found that the definition was still in use and was contributing to a considerable under-estimate of the number of black children in schools. Furthermore, the then Secretary of State for Education and Science, Margaret Thatcher, told the Committee: 'My department makes no use of them whatsoever except to publish them. They do not form the basis of any grant from my department.' The Committee concluded that the statistics had served 'little or no practical purpose' and recommended that their collection should cease forthwith (Select Committee on Race Relations and Immigration, 1973). The collection of the information was stopped the same year.

After 1973 there was no systematic collection of data on the numbers of black, that is Asian or Afro-Caribbean, children in schools or their progress and experience in school, including performance in examinations. No data were collected on the numbers of black teachers or their promotion (or lack of it). Nor were any data collected on what happened to black pupils after they left school. Did they go on to university or polytechnic, or to colleges to improve their school qualifications? Were they more likely to follow certain paths than others, more or less likely to take certain routes than their white counterparts? Without data it was impossible to answer these questions.

Calls for the reintroduction of ethnic monitoring in schools by bodies such as the Select Committee on Race Relations and Immigration (see 1977a), the CRE, the Inner London Education Authority (ILEA) and the National Union of Teachers, went unheeded. In addition, the lack of data was a problem which faced the Committee of Inquiry into the Education of Children from Ethnic Minority Groups set up in 1979 as a result of increasing disquiet about the relative under-achievement of many black pupils in schools. This was chaired initially by Anthony Rampton, and then by Lord Swann. In its interim report, *West Indian Children in Our Schools*, the Rampton Committee said that, while some schools collected ethnic data, there was little uniformity in the classifications used and it was difficult to make any meaningful comparisons between schools, let alone gain an overall picture. The Committee had said that ethnically-based statistics could be of use to central government in determining national education policy; to local education authorities in quantifying and locating particular needs; to schools so that they could take full account of the cultural and linguistic backgrounds of pupils and see whether any groups were under-achieving or were disproportionately represented in any subject or class; and to parents so they could assess their children's performances in relation to their peers. The Committee recommended the ethnic monitoring of pupils and of trainee and qualified teachers. It also recommended ethnic monitoring in higher education, an area in which information on the racial composition of student populations (apart from overseas students) and staff and their progress was even more sparse than in schools (Rampton, 1981; DES, 1985).

Following this recommendation, a working group was convened by the DES to consider how this might be put into practice and in 1989 the government announced that, with effect from September 1990, all local education authority and grant-maintained schools would be required to collect ethnically-based data on their pupils (DES, 1989; Scottish Education Department, 1989). The government accepted the working party's conclusion that the collection of such statistics would be of great benefit to schools and education authorities in making appropriate provision and in monitoring progress. The working party recommended, and the government accepted, that information should be provided on a voluntary basis on three subjects: ethnic origin, categorized as white, black-African, black-Caribbean, black-other, Indian, Pakistani, Bangladeshi, Chinese, and other; language, involving thirteen categories; and religious affiliations. It was proposed that this information be collected during interviews with parents about the admission of children. The circular anticipated that a full profile of the school population would take four years. After this, the Department of Education and Science said, it would also require returns to be made on the destinations of pupils leaving school and on examination results at 16 and 18.

In the same year, the DES announced that from January 1990, education authorities in England and Wales would be required to submit returns on the ethnic origins of school teachers. This will use the same categories as used in relation to school pupils and will also record details of seniority, pay and specialization. The collection of such data, Kenneth Baker, then Education Secretary, said, was essential to measure the success of efforts to increase the numbers of minority ethnic group school teachers. (There is no comparable monitoring in Scotland.) In the case of further and higher education, systematic ethnic monitoring was to start from November 1990 (the academic year 1990–1) for universities and polytechnics. Again this applies only to England and Wales and the Scottish universities.

Such monitoring will reveal a great deal, not just about bare numbers but also about the progress of black children through school, the examinations for which they are entered, the results achieved and their destinations after leaving school. It will also show how these compare with their white counterparts. In identifying any significant differences such monitoring may also be identifying ways in which the treatment of black pupils in schools may discriminate against them. In the case of teachers, the monitoring will highlight not just the numbers of black teachers but their grades and positions and, again, will help to highlight possibly discriminatory mechanisms.

This brief case study illustrates the point made earlier: that the collection of data involves decisions about what is being looked for, about the purpose of statistics. The experience of the collection of data on 'immigrant pupils' between 1966 and 1973, in particular, showed how the fact of collecting information could contribute to the definition of black people as a problem and how it could be used to their disadvantage in that it was the number of black pupils in individual schools that was officially regarded as the source of the social problem. It also shows that data collected for one purpose cannot always be easily transferred to another purpose. In this case, the problems related to the presence of Asian and Afro-Caribbean children in schools were initially seen as being related to the problems of immigration. But as an increasing proportion of such pupils were British-born, the problem could no longer be seen as one of immigration but one of colour. The basis of the monitoring system remained unchanged and became less and less accurate and increasingly useless as the years passed.

The re-introduction of ethnic monitoring in schools, of staff as well as pupils, coupled with the extension of monitoring into the areas of further education, teacher training, and universities and polytechnics, stemmed from a growing dissatisfaction among minority ethnic group communities. This was reflected in the reports of the influential government-created committee into the education of minority ethnic group children (Rampton, 1981; DES, 1985). It stemmed also from a recognition among politicians and other policy-makers, particularly after the 1981 urban disorders, that continuing racial discrimination and inequality and the resultant exclusion from society of a section of the population, could have seriously disruptive effects.

Conclusion

Statistical information can play an important role in identifying patterns of inequality and the processes that produce them. The data which emerge, for example, from ethnic monitoring in education ought to point to the ways in which black people, whether pupils or teachers, are treated differently from their white counterparts. It is important to keep in mind, however, that statistics do not just reflect facts which are 'out there' waiting to be discovered, but are the result of many decisions and, of course, can be open to very different interpretations.

The limits of statistics

While acknowledging the importance that statistical information *can* have, it is important to keep in mind that this is only one form of information. It is not necessarily superior to other forms of evidence and may, indeed, be inappropriate. The problems of human beings cannot always be quantified and even when they can they may not be best described in this way. The example with which I began is a case in point. There is a sense in which attempting to quantify the problem of racial violence misses the meaning of such violence for those who are affected, whether they are actually victims or simply fear that they may be attacked. The case study or history or open interview may well yield more information and prove more illuminating of a particular problem than bare numerical data. As an example, we might contrast the many papers and articles written on the number of black people in mental hospitals with a report on the experiences of black people in the mental health system (Westwood *et al.*, 1989). The former yield data which is, to be sure, important and necessary, but the latter goes behind the statistics to illuminate the human experience and thus adds to our under-standing of the processes behind the patterns.

Central to any discussion of statistics is, of course, the uses to which they are put. There is little value in collecting information simply for its own sake (undoubtedly a tendency in bureaucratic societies) and this is particularly true when the subjects of such data collection are human beings. As we have seen, many people have objected to being the object of study, research or simply counting when they have been unable to see any benefits that might accrue. They have argued that a considerable amount of research has been conducted and a vast amount of data accumulated in the last 30 years pointing to the existence of discrimination on a wide scale and to the continuing subordinate position of black people, socially and economically and that this has given rise to very little by way of action to alter the situation in any significant way.

The collection of ethnic data is not an end in itself but a means to an end: that of implementing equal opportunities and racial equality. The current support for ethnic monitoring in education, as well as in other areas, indicates a willingness to take at least the first steps in this process by identifying the ways in which minority ethnic groups may be discriminated against. But it must be remembered that these are first steps only. They will have to be followed, where the data shows it to be necessary, by changes in policy and practice.

PART 2

MINORITY ETHNIC GROUPS IN THE UK: A PROFILE

Richard Skellington, assisted by Paulette Morris

1 DEMOGRAPHIC TRENDS AMONGST GREAT BRITAIN'S MINORITY ETHNIC GROUP POPULATION

1.1 Introduction: a note of caution

In compiling this dossier, we hesitated before deciding to include a section on demographic trends. We did not want to reinforce stereotypes or exacerbate a sense of 'otherness' between ethnic groups. We did feel, however, that some population details about minority ethnic groups in Britain would leave readers better informed, particularly in relation to differences between the groups themselves, and to the importance of age differences between population cohorts.

Details about the British minority ethnic group population are best derived from Labour Force Surveys (LFS). In the summer of 1990, LFS figures summarizing the surveys of 1986, 1987 and 1988 were published. The three-year average represents a far more reliable estimate of the British minority ethnic group population than annual snapshots.[1]

1.2 Population size

According to the LFS, almost one person in twenty living in Great Britain belongs to a minority ethnic group. For the period 1986–8, the LFS estimated the minority ethnic group population to be 2.58 million, or 4.7 per cent of the total British population. This represented an increase of half a million on their estimate for 1981, and more than double the minority ethnic group population of 1971. Of these 2.58 million, about 1 million are Muslims.

This book was written before minority ethnic group data from the 1991 census was known. (That census will provide a more detailed picture.) *Figure 1.1* shows the age and place of birth of the black and Asian population of England and Wales enumerated by the census of 1981.

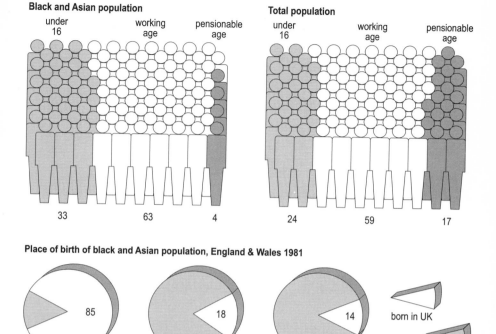

Figure 1.1: age and place of birth of population, England and Wales, 1981
(Adapted from Fothergill and Vincent, 1985, p. 14)

A comparison of LFS estimates with census findings shows that the minority ethnic group population has grown from 0.4 per cent in 1951, 1 per cent in 1961, 2.3 per cent in 1971, to 3.9 per cent in 1981 (see *Figure 1.2*). During the 1980s the total British minority ethnic group population increased at around 80–90,000 per year (OPCS, 1986; Shaw, 1988b). *Figure 1.3* provides a breakdown of the percentage of the total British population for different minority ethnic groups. *Figure 1.4* shows the percentage of the total minority ethnic group population belonging to each group. Over a half (51 per cent) of the total minority ethnic group population were of Indian, Pakistani or Bangladeshi origin, almost a fifth were of West Indian origin, while one in nine were of mixed ethnic origin. Between 1981 and 1988 the Pakistani population was estimated to have grown by a half and the Bangladeshi population to have doubled, whereas the West Indian population declined by 33,000 during the same period. *Table 1.1* analyses these trends. LFS findings show that West Indian families have fewer and Pakistani and Bangladeshi families more dependent children than the average minority ethnic group family (see Section 1.3).

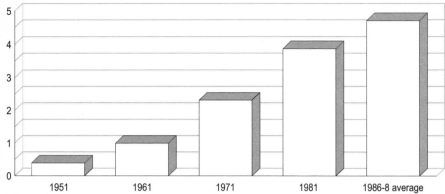

Figure 1.2: percentage growth in the British minority ethnic group populations 1951–88
(Adapted from OPCS and LFS)

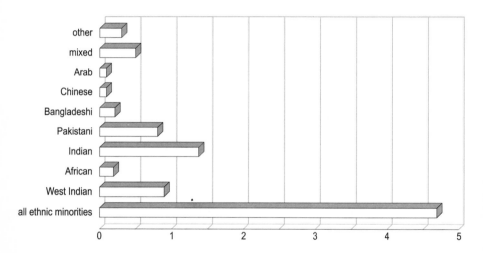

Figure 1.3: percentage of the total British population of each minority ethnic group
(Adapted from LFS, average 1986–8)

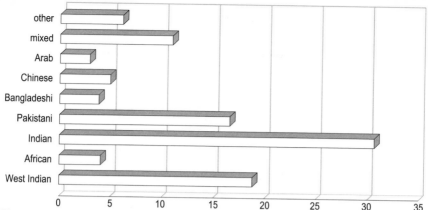

Figure 1.4: minority ethnic group populations as a percentage of the total minority ethnic group population of Great Britain
(Adapted from LFS, average 1986–8)

Table 1.1: estimated growth and decline in minority ethnic group populations

	1981	1986–8 average
West Indian	528,000	495,000
African	80,000	112,000
Indian	727,000	787,000
Pakistani	284,000	428,000
Bangladeshi	52,000	108,000
Chinese	92,000	125,000
Arab	53,000	73,000
Mixed	217,000	287,000
Other	60,000	164,000
All minority ethnic groups	2,092,000	2,577,000

(Adapted from LFS, 1981, 1986, 1987 and 1988)

Variations in the growth (or decline) of minority ethnic group populations are related to stages in the life cycle. *Figure 1.5* shows the LFS estimates of the British population aged under ten. Considerable variation is revealed: 30 per cent of the Pakistani population, 34 per cent of the Bangladeshi, and 40 per cent of those of mixed ethnic origin were children aged under ten (compared with 17 per cent for the West Indian population and 12 per cent for the white). The LFS estimates reveal that at least nine in every ten minority ethnic group children aged under five were born in the UK.

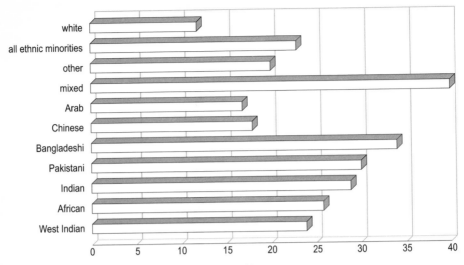

Figure 1.5: percentage of the population under 10
(Adapted from LFS, 1986)

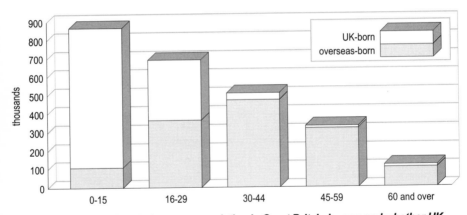

Figure 1.6: the minority ethnic group population in Great Britain by age and whether UK born or overseas born
(Adapted from Central Statistical Office, 1991, p. 25)

Further analysis of the 1984–6 LFS averages showed that more than one in three of the British minority ethnic group population was younger than 16. *Social Trends 21* revealed marked differences in age structure between UK-born and overseas-born members of the minority ethnic group population (see *Figure 1.6*). Two-thirds of the minority ethnic group population born in the UK were aged under 16 and only one in twenty were aged over 29. In contrast, only 8 per cent of the overseas-born population were aged under 16, while almost two-thirds were aged over 29. Most of the overseas-born arrived in the UK as young adults, or as dependents, while those born within the UK were the first or subsequent generation of migrants (Central Statistical Office, 1991, p. 25). These distinct age distributions are related to length of residence in the UK and to the cycle of migration.

1.3 Household and family data: size and composition

LFS averages for 1985–7 showed that three-quarters of Pakistani and Bangladeshi households and three-fifths of Indian households contained four or more people, compared with a quarter of white households (Central Statistical Office, 1990a)[2] (see *Figure 1.7*). *Figure 1.8* reveals the average number of persons per household for each ethnic group.

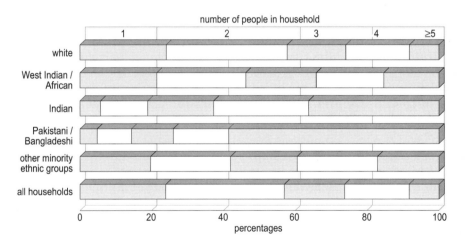

Figure 1.7: household size in Great Britain by ethnic group of head of household, 1985-7 *(Adapted from Central Statistical Office, 1990a, p. 36)*

In 1988 over a quarter of all households in Britain contained only one person, compared to one in eight in 1961; the proportion was higher for white and West Indian/African populations than for Indian, Pakistani and Bangladeshi groups. During the same period the proportion of households containing five or more people has halved. In 1988 it was less than one in twelve, while the average household size reduced from 3.09 to 2.48 people.

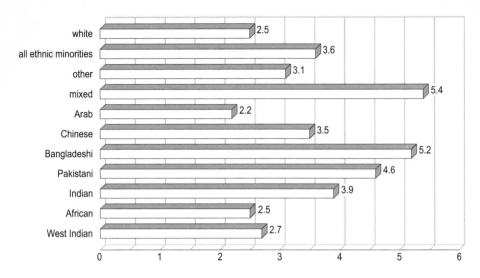

Figure 1.8: average number of persons per household in Great Britain by ethnic group
(Adapted from LFS, 1985-7)

These data are crucially related to a variety of factors such as the age structure of the different groups, fertility rates, household composition and cultural influences. Minority ethnic group households, particularly Asian households, contain greater proportions of families with children and smaller proportions of people living on their own. LFS averages for 1985–7, for example, reveal over 40 per cent of Pakistani, Bangladeshi and mixed origin populations to be under 16.[3]

Analysis of minority ethnic group family sizes reveals significant differences between ethnic groups. For example, on average, there are three people in each white family and just under four in each minority ethnic group family.[4] *Figure 1.9* shows the mean family size by ethnic group of the family head and *Figure 1.10* the numbers of dependent children per family.[5]

The figures show that:

1   The proportion of lone-parent families was highest among West Indian families (44 per cent). For other groups the figures were: 33 per cent for 'mixed' ethnic origin, 27 per cent for African, 6 per cent for both Indian and Pakistani, 5 per cent for Bangladeshi and 11 per cent for white families. About every other West Indian family was a one-parent family compared to every third African and mixed ethnic origin family. The prevalance of one-parent families among Indian, Pakistani and Bangladeshi groups was well below that of white families (Haskey, 1991b, p. 39).[6]

    Three observations should be noted. First, West Indian families account for less than 1 per cent of all families in Britain. Second, in

1987, 14 per cent of all families with dependent children in Britain were headed by lone parents, which is twice the proportion found in 1971. Third, it is estimated that over six out of every ten one-parent families are living in or on the margins of poverty, compared with two out of ten two-parent families (Family Policy Studies Centre, 1986; Central Statistical Office, 1991, p. 35).

2 37 per cent of all West Indian families were headed by a female, compared to 9 per cent of white families.

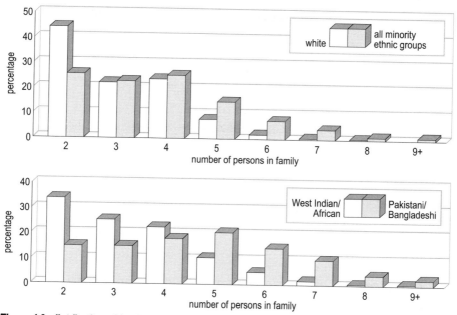

Figure 1.9: distribution of family size in Great Britain by ethnic group of head of family, 1985–7 *(Adapted from Haskey, 1989, p. 12)*

Fertility rates fell in England and Wales between 1971 and 1981, and have since remained relatively stable. However, fertility rates for overseas-born women have in general continued to decline. The proportion of births to mothers born in the New Commonwealth and Pakistan (NCWP) fell during the 1980s, from 7.8 per cent in 1981 to 6.8 per cent in 1989.[7]

To summarize the LFS findings, West Indian, African, Chinese, Arab minority ethnic groups and the white majority population share several characteristics: smaller numbers of people and families per household, fewer dependent children per family, and a smaller proportion of households containing extended families. Indian, Pakistani and Bangladeshi populations have followed these broad trends but are still far more likely to live within extended families.

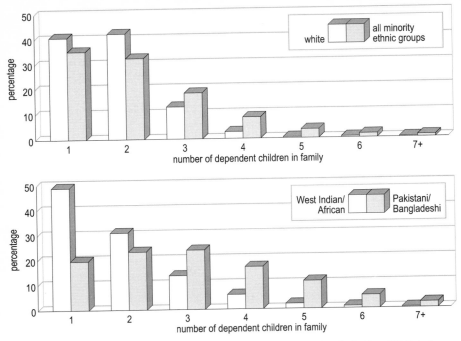

Figure 1.10: distribution of numbers of dependent children per family in Great Britain by ethnic group of head of family, 1985–7
(Adapted from Haskey, 1989, p. 12)

1.4 Location, concentration and segregation

Britain's minority ethnic group population is largely urban and is character-ized by residential segregation. Only 3 per cent of black and Asian residents (in contrast to the national average of 24 per cent) live in rural enumeration districts, while 75 per cent live in a set of urban enumeration districts which contain only 10 per cent of whites.[8] Half the white population in Britain live in towns and rural areas that have less than half of one per cent of their residents coming from minority ethnic groups. Only about one in sixteen white people live in an enumeration district with a black and Asian population of 5 per cent or more, although these areas accommodate 60 per cent of all minority ethnic group populations. The 1980s began with a higher proportion of black people living in the most segregated urban areas than did the 1970s (Brown, 1984, p. 20).

Maps 1.1 to *1.5* show the regional distribution of each of Britain's minority ethnic group populations towards the end of the 1980s.[9] The highest concentrations live in London and Birmingham, while the lowest are in non-metropolitan counties, especially in the South West, the North and Wales.

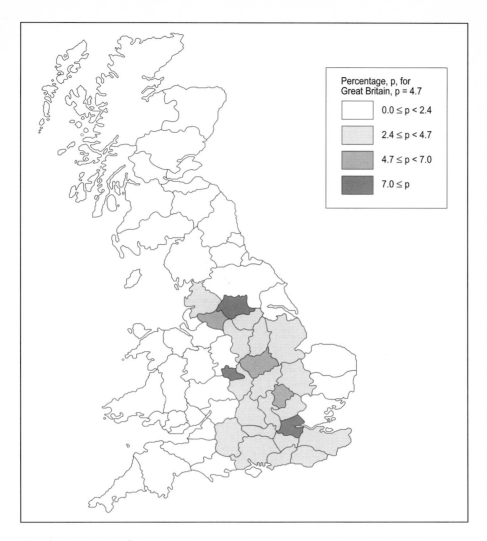

*Map 1.1: estimated minority ethnic group population as a percentage of the total
population, by county or region, 1986–8*
(Haskey, 1991a, p. 28)

One in six residents in Greater London and the West Midlands is either
Asian, Afro-Caribbean, Chinese or of mixed 'race', according to OPCS
estimates (1991). These estimates of minority ethnic group populations
revealed that Birmingham has the largest populations of West Indians,
Pakistanis and Indians, with 36,100, 39,700 and 49,800 respectively, the
London borough of Lambeth the largest African population, with 7,700;
Tower Hamlets the largest Bangladeshi population, with 18,100; West-
minster the largest Chinese population, with 3,600; and Kensington and
Chelsea the largest Arab population, with 3,500. The London borough of
Brent has the highest proportion of minority ethnic group population – 27
per cent.

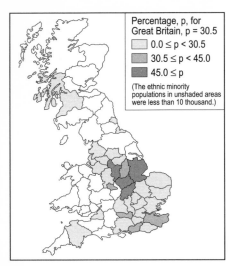

Percentage, p, for
Great Britain, p = 30.5

☐ 0.0 ≤ p < 30.5
▨ 30.5 ≤ p < 45.0
▨ 45.0 ≤ p

(The ethnic minority
populations in unshaded areas
were less than 10 thousand.)

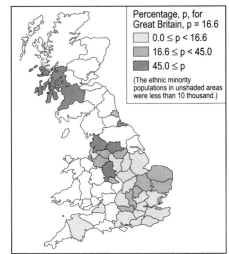

Percentage, p, for
Great Britain, p = 16.6

☐ 0.0 ≤ p < 16.6
▨ 16.6 ≤ p < 45.0
▨ 45.0 ≤ p

(The ethnic minority
populations in unshaded areas
were less than 10 thousand.)

Map 1.2: estimated percentage of the minority ethnic group population of Indian origin, by county or region, 1986–8

Map 1.3: estimated percentage of the minority ethnic group population of Pakistani origin, by county or region, 1986–8

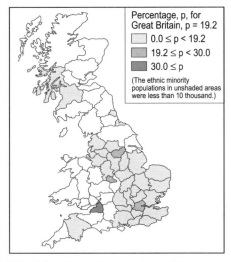

Percentage, p, for
Great Britain, p = 19.2

☐ 0.0 ≤ p < 19.2
▨ 19.2 ≤ p < 30.0
▨ 30.0 ≤ p

(The ethnic minority
populations in unshaded areas
were less than 10 thousand.)

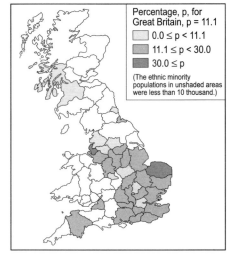

Percentage, p, for
Great Britain, p = 11.1

☐ 0.0 ≤ p < 11.1
▨ 11.1 ≤ p < 30.0
▨ 30.0 ≤ p

(The ethnic minority
populations in unshaded areas
were less than 10 thousand.)

Map 1.4: estimated percentage of the minority ethnic group population of West Indian origin, by county or region, 1986–8

Map 1.5: estimated percentage of the minority ethnic group population of mixed ethnic origin, by county or region, 1986–8

(Haskey 1991a, p. 30)

Table 1.2: metropolitan districts, London boroughs and non-metropolitan counties with the twelve largest minority ethnic group populations, 1986–8, in thousands

	West Indian/Guyanese		African		Indian		Pakistani		Bangladeshi		Chinese		Arab		Mixed	
	Area	Pop.	Area	Pop.	Area	Pop.	Area	Pop.	Area	Pop.	Area	Pop.	Area	Pop.	Area	Pop.
1	Birmingham	36.1	Lambeth	7.7	Birmingham	49.8	Birmingham	39.7	Tower Hamlets	18.1	Westminster	3.6	Kensington and Chelsea	3.5	Hampshire	7.1
2	Lambeth	23.9	Wandsworth	7.1	Leicestershire	41.6	Bradford	32.2	Birmingham	9.9	Hampshire	3.5	Westminster	3.5	Kent	6.9
3	Wandsworth	20.0	Haringay	6.0	Ealing	36.6	Lancashire	22.4	Bedfordshire	3.5	Barnet	3.2	Camden	2.5	Essex	6.7
4	Lewisham	19.9	Hackney	5.3	Brent	32.4	Leeds	17.5	Camden	3.0	Ealing	3.0	Barnet	2.2	Birmingham	6.4
5	Hackney	18.5	Southwark	4.8	Hounslow	21.7	Kirklees	16.3	Newcastle-upon-Tyne	2.8	Brent	3.0	Birmingham	1.8	Wandsworth	5.8
6	Southwark	17.9	Newham	4.6	Barnet	21.5	Manchester	10.5	Hackney	2.7	Camden	2.9	Liverpool	1.5	Lambeth	5.5
7	Haringey	17.7	Lewisham	4.4	Harrow	19.8	Glasgow	8.9	Sandwell	2.5	Essex	2.6	Haringey	1.5	Lewisham	5.4
8	Brent	16.5	Islington	3.9	Croydon	19.2	Newham	8.5	Bradford	2.4	Kent	2.6	South Glamorgan	1.5	Surrey	5.0
9	Newham	15.9	Westminster	3.5	Coventry	17.9	Berkshire	7.6	Westminster	2.4	Surrey	2.3	Wandsworth	1.4	Southwark	4.8
10	Hammersmith and Fulham	11.1	Brent	3.3	Wolverhampton	17.5	Calderdale	7.2	Southwark	2.3	Kensington and Chelsea	2.2	Lambeth	1.3	Newham	4.8
11	Islington	11.0	Camden	3.1	Sandwell	17.4	Wakefield	7.0	Wandsworth	2.3	Haringey	2.2	Hammersmith and Fulham	1.3	Hertfordshire	4.7
12	Westminster	9.7	Hammersmith and Fulham	2.9	Derbyshire	15.2	Staffordshire	7.0	Lambeth	2.2	Wandsworth	2.1	Hackney	1.3	Haringey	4.6

(Haskey, 1991a, p. 34)

Table 1.2 shows the metropolitan districts, London boroughs and non-metropolitan counties with the twelve largest minority ethnic group populations for each minority ethnic group studied by the LFS in 1986–8.

The concentration of black and Asian minority ethnic groups also affects their parliamentary representation. Estimates in 1987 indicated that 100 constituencies in England have a black population of over 10 per cent: of these, half were considered marginal. Had Parliament been truly representative in the 1987 General Election, there would have been at least 30 black MPs elected, not six.[10]

1.5 Future trends

In 1979 projections indicated that by the year 2000 the NCWP-origin population of Britain would be in the region of 3.3 million (OPCS, 1979). This estimate was based on trends in births and deaths, and on the levels of immigration and emigration then current. This would mean that about 1 in 17, or 5.9 per cent, of the total population of Britain would be black. Further immigration restrictions would, of course, be expected to reduce the number of immigrants. However, even if all immigration of NCWP citizens were to cease, OPCS calculated that their estimate for the year 2000 would be reduced by only 0.6 million. After the year 2000, OPCS expected the proportion of black people in the total population of Britain to stabilize at around 6 per cent, because of low net migration and a gradual levelling out of demographic differences in age patterns and relative affluence between populations (Runnymede Trust and RSRG, 1980, pp. 27–8).

Notes

1   Since LFS data are widely used in *'Race' in Britain Today*, an explanation of how the data are gathered is appropriate. The LFS is conducted each spring. The survey covers approximately 60,000 private households containing about 150,000 individuals. Respondents are shown a card listing a number of minority ethnic groups and asked to say to which group they consider they belong. The response rate is around 80 per cent each year, and approximately 7,000 of successful interviews are conducted with members of minority ethnic group populations. The LFS minority ethnic group definitions are: West Indian or Guyanese, Indian, Pakistani, Bangladeshi, Chinese, African, Arab, mixed origin, and other.

In this section on demographic trends, LFS definitions are used unless specified otherwise: the term 'white' comes from LFS. LFS data are presented from annual surveys between 1985 and 1989. For demographic trend data, *Social Trends 20* (Central Statistical Office, 1990a) remains the main source, backed up by detailed OPCS analyses of earlier LFS three-year averages, and the Haskey analysis published in spring 1991 (see below). Later sections have incorporated labour market data from the surveys of 1986–9, and from *Social Trends 21* (Central Statistical Office, 1991).

For a detailed analysis of the minority ethnic group population resident in private households in England and Wales only, based on LFS data from 1986 to 1988, see John Haskey's analysis of county and metropolitan data (1991a).

2 LFS definitions of a household are used here. A household refers to a group of co-resident individuals who share certain space within a dwelling.

3 A detailed discussion of the demography of minority ethnic group household and family data can be found in Haskey (1989). Haskey's data were based on rough estimates pending the outcome of the 1991 census results. For an analysis of lone-parent trends see Haskey (1991b).

4 Haskey's definition of a family comprised either a married couple on their own, or a married couple/lone parent and their never-married children, provided these children have no children of their own within the household.

5 Dependent children here refers to either those aged under 16 years, or those aged 16–18 (inclusive) who have never married and are either in full-time education or on a government scheme.

6 Haskey's definition of a lone parent is wider in scope than the standard definition and includes lone parents with non-dependent children. Neither his interpretation nor those included in official statistics mentions cohabitation: the proportion of lone-parent families discussed here is therefore an under-representation for *all* groups.

7 See Central Statistical Office (1991) pp. 28–9. These trends reflect changes in the number of women of childbearing age born in different parts of the world. But, increasingly, mothers from minority ethnic groups in the younger childbearing ages are themselves born in Britain and births to such women are now included in the category of mothers born in the United Kingdom. Categorized by country of birth of mother, the data for 1989 show that the estimated fertility rate for mothers born in the UK was 1.8 and for mothers born in NCWP 2.7.

8 Here 'black' and 'white' refer to the categories used by the Policy Studies Institute (PSI) in their 1982 national survey of multi-racial Britain (Brown, 1984).

9 See Haskey (1991a) pp. 28–31 and Smith (1989) p. 30. The 1991 census will clarify the extent to which Britain has become more segregated during the 1980s. Smith's definition 'black' merges LFS minority ethnic group categories used in 1985 to 1987.

Both Haskey and Smith exclude Northern Ireland from their maps and analyses.

10 Reported on BBC Radio 4, *The Black Vote in Britain*, 14 April 1990.

2 IMMIGRATION

2.1 Introduction: the politics of control

Immigration policy is central to understanding racism in British society. British governments have long sought to control immigration. In 1985, reporting their formal investigation into immigration procedures, the Commission for Racial Equality (CRE) concluded:

> The way in which the [immigration] controls developed, and all the surrounding debate and controversy, made the issue as much one of race as of immigration *per se*, and there have been several opposing views about what are acceptable objectives for immigration control policies. At one extreme has been the view that the efficiency and effectiveness of the controls can be judged almost solely on their success in reducing and restricting the numbers of black people admitted for settlement. At the other has been the view that the legislation has been racist and that the governments responsible have pandered to racist attitudes in society, even encouraging and exacerbating them, rather than seeking to eradicate them.
>
> (CRE, 1985a, p. 126)

Politicians have focused on controlling entry to the United Kingdom by imposing restrictive legislation, particularly upon black Commonwealth migrants and their dependents. In 1989, the Runnymede Trust concluded:

> Black people are a problem and unwelcome here. That is the message which is restated and reaffirmed every time immigration policy is made more restrictive. It is a message not lost on 'our people' in Britain – on the employers who can ask, with reason, why they should have 'them' in their firm if the government does not want them in the country, on the tenants who do not want them in 'their' streets or housing estates, on the parents and pupils who do not want them in 'their' schools, on the 42 per cent of young white people who, according to the *British Social Attitudes Survey*, will now willingly admit to racial prejudice.
>
> (Gordon, 1989a, p. 13)

To most politicians, immigration controls have been a necessary corollary of 'good relations'. The political rhetoric justifying the necessity for immigration control can potentially have the effect of institutionalizing racism and, through the use of emotive language and imagery, reinforce the commonsense assumptions which have kept racism flourishing in British society. The extracts below represent a cross-section of mainstream political statements on immigration since the end of the Second World War:

> An influx of coloured people domiciled here is likely to impair the harmony, strength and cohesion of our public and social life and to cause discord and unhappiness among all concerned.

(Letter to Clement Attlee signed by eleven Labour MPs, 1948)[1]

> I believe that unrestricted immigration can only produce additional problems, additional suffering and additional hardship unless some kind of limitation is imposed and continued ... there is an economic necessity to have a certain amount of immigration but a social reason for control.

(Roy Hattersley, *Hansard*, 1965)

> The main purpose of immigration policy ... is a contribution to peace and harmony ... If we are to get progress in community relations, we must give assurance to the people, who were already here before the large wave of immigration, that this will be the end and that there will be no further large-scale immigration. Unless we can give that assurance, we cannot effectively set about improving community relations.

(Reginald Maudling, 1971, cited in MacDonald, 1983, pp. 16–17)

> People are really rather afraid that this country might be rather swamped by people with a different culture ... the British character has done so much for democracy, for law, and done so much throughout the world, that if there is any fear that it might be swamped, people are going to react and be rather hostile to those coming in. So if you want good race relations, you've got to allay people's fears on numbers.

(Margaret Thatcher, 1978)[2]

> It would not be in the interests of the ethnic minorities themselves if there were a prospect of further mass inward movement. That prospect would increase social tensions, particularly in our cities. That is why we say that firm immigration control is essential if we are to have good community relations.

(Douglas Hurd, Secretary of State at the Home Office, *Hansard*, 1987)

2.2 The historical context

Of the major migrations to Britain during the last 150 years, three are of particular demographic and political significance, especially in relation to statistics and control: Irish migration since 1840, East European Jewish migration before the First World War, and migrants from the New Commonwealth after the Second World War.[3]

Until 1844 British citizenship was only possible to an 'immigrant' by means of a private Act of Parliament. Since then, legislation has been introduced to exclude 'aliens' or 'foreign citizens' or 'immigrants' from entering the country. A range of reasons lay behind immigration legislation: the protection of the labour market or the existing social composition, the exclusion of individuals considered undesirable on political or criminal grounds, or – as in the five statements quoted above – the maintainance of 'good' 'race' or community relations, or to facilitate 'integration'.

The Naturalisation Act of 1870, for example, introduced a five-year residential qualification; the Aliens Act of 1905 controlled the flow of Jewish migrants into Britain; the British Nationality and Status of Aliens Act of 1914 introduced 'good character' criteria, while the 1920 Aliens Order provided the basis for control until 1971. From 1920, 'foreign citizens', as 'aliens' were now called, were obliged to complete landing and embarkation cards. These records formed and informed legislative change until the 1960s.

2.3 Migration statistics and measurement

Much early immigration policy was introduced on the basis of almost non-existent statistics and, where data were available, they were often based on inadequate definitions and measurement. In 1905, before the passage of the Aliens Act of that year, Bonar Law, answering a parliamentary question seeking statistics on immigration from 1895–1904, replied: 'I regret I am not in a position to give this information'.[4]

Immigration statistics have invariably been produced as a by-product of exercising control, rather than used to assess whether further legislation, and of what kind, is necessary. The often heated political debates about numbers and projections that have characterized much parliamentary debate on immigration, have often had the effect of triggering further immigration flows of people fearing an increase in controls on entry in the future.

There are obstacles to the collection of reliable immigration statistics. One is scale. For example, in 1985, 37 million people entered Britain from overseas (about the same number left). Of these 37 million, only an estimated 200,000 were intending immigrants (that is, people who stated an intention of staying for twelve months or more); 8.5 million were subject to full immigration control; 6 million were EC citizens; and the other 22.5 million, mostly UK citizens, were not subject to immigration control. In 1985, over 74 million people arrived in and/or left the UK, a number greater than the population of England and Wales and 50 times the number of births and deaths in any year (see Coleman, 1987, pp. 1140–1).

2.4 The IPS and Home Office statistics

Until 1961 the only official statistics on immigrants came from passenger statistics collected by the Board of Trade. In 1961 a voluntary survey was established. Drawing on a 5 per cent sample of arrivals and departures, it formed the basis of the International Passenger Survey (IPS).[5] One limitation of the IPS is that intending immigrants form only a small fraction of the traffic flow (in 1964, for example, they comprised only 1.3 per cent of arrival interviews and about 2 per cent of departure interviews). In the IPS, information on movement from countries involved in substantial migration flows to Britain is based on only a few hundred interviews. So, for example, the figure of 26,000 estimated Australian immigrants in 1975 was based on 479 interviews, and the estimated 23,000 from all the EC countries on only 91 (OPCS, 1978; Coleman, 1987, p. 1152). In general, the IPS permits too much interpretation to be based on responses from too few people.[6]

Home Office statistics analyse acceptances for settlement by nationality. They are based on information on the landing card: name, birth-place, date of birth, nationality, occupation, sex, UK address and details of arrival or departure. No analysis of these variables by acceptances is published in the annual *Control of Immigration Statistics*. The published data deal only with arrivals: an annual statistical bulletin on immigration from the Indian sub-continent provides additional information on age of children on entry, year of marriage and year of entry of spouse (Home Office, 1985; Home Affairs Committee, 1985).

Information on acceptance for settlement by nationality can be found in the *Control of Immigration Statistics Annual Abstract of Statistics* and, occasionally, in *Social Trends*. Figures for 1990 showed that 52,400 people were accepted for settlement: a quarter of these were from the Indian sub-continent and a further 20 per cent from the rest of Asia (Home Office, 1991). This was considerably less than the 80,750 admitted in 1976.

Contemporary migration statistics tend to be asymmetrical and record the flow of incoming persons – so, for example, detailed analysis of the kinds of persons return-migrating is not available. There is no control of emigration from the UK and thus no Home Office emigration figures. IPS figures are the only source on emigration data.[7]

> Home Office statistics do not treat immigration in a demographically very useful way. They measure flows only in one direction, provide no demographic or socio-economic characteristics on those accepted for settlement … At present they add nothing to our social or demographic picture of the immigrant population of the UK.

(Coleman, 1987, p. 1162)

2.5 The British-born minority ethnic group population

Immigrants represent a declining proportion of Britain's minority ethnic group population. Nine out of every ten minority ethnic group children aged under 5 were born in the UK. In 1984 the third PSI survey estimated that 40 per cent of Britain's black population was British born; moreover, PSI further estimated that 50 per cent of those who came to Britain as immigrants had lived in Britain for over fifteen years (Brown, 1984, p. 2).

2.6 The importance of 'white' immigration

The word 'immigrant' is often wrongly used to refer only to black people. The majority of immigrants are white – from Eire or the Old Commonwealth (Australia, New Zealand and Canada) or from other European countries. The 1981 census, for example, revealed that nearly 3.4 million people in Britain were born overseas. Of these, 1.9 million were white – 607,000 were born in Ireland, 153,000 in the Old Commonwealth and about 1.13 million in other countries including Western Europe.[8] The remainder, 1.41 million, were born in the New Commonwealth and Pakistan (NCWP). A further 100,000 white people were born in the Indian sub-continent and East Africa while their parents were on overseas service.

2.7 The importance of emigration

Britain is traditionally a net exporter of people. Between 1971 and 1983, more people left Britain than came in. Overall the net loss of population during this period was 465,000, mainly as a result of emigration to Australia, Canada, New Zealand, the USA, South Africa and the EC. In 1988 the net loss was 21,000. NCWP immigration, substantial though it has been, has helped reverse the overall pattern to give a net population gain from migration only in the years 1962, 1972 and 1983–5. Taking the minority ethnic group population alone, analysis of LFS data has revealed a net gain of around 30,000 migrants each year to the UK population: about 24,000 of these come from NCWP countries (Shaw, 1988b, p. 29).

2.8 Migration from the New Commonwealth and Pakistan

Since 1962 successive governments have passed laws to control NCWP immigration. The 1981 British Nationality Act introduced a tiered system of citizenship. It gave several million existing 'partial' citizens (i.e. those with UK-born grandparents – almost all white) the same right of abode in the UK as British citizens had. At the same time, British dependent territories' citizens, British overseas citizens, British protected persons and British subjects without citizenship of any Commonwealth country had no right of abode under the Act. The majority of people in these categories are of Indian, Chinese, Afro-Caribbean or other non-European descent (Nanda, 1988, p. 270; Action Group on Immigration and Nationality and Immigrations Laws, n.d., pp. 2–3).

The 1962, 1968, 1971 and 1988 immigration acts considerably reduced the inflow of migrants. Total immigration from NCWP countries has declined substantially from 136,000 in 1961 and 68,000 in 1972 to 22,800 in 1988. In 1988 citizens from the NCWP accounted for 46.3 per cent of the total acceptances for settlement in the UK (see *Table 2.1* and *Figure 2.1*).

Table 2.1: acceptances for settlement in Great Britain by nationality, 1984–8

All nationalities	1984 50,950 %	1985 55,360 %	1986 46,980 %	1987 45,980 %	1988 49,280 %
Foreign	47.6	46.5	50.1	48.2	47.4
Commonwealth	52.4	51.5	49.9	51.8	52.6
NCWP	48.7	48.9	47.4	45.3	46.3
Old Commonwealth	14.6	14.7	13.8	15.1	15.0

(Central Statistical Office, 1990b)

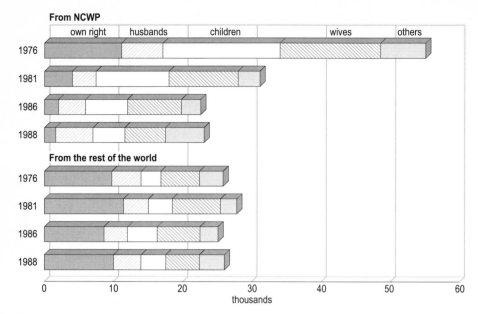

Figure 2.1: acceptances for settlement in Great Britain by category of acceptance
(Adapted from Central Statistical Office, 1990a)

The 1971 Immigration Act imposed strict controls on the entry of males seeking work. Primary immigration (men accepted for settlement on arrival) peaked in 1972 at 18,000, fell to 6,400 in 1983, and is now confined to people with job skills in short supply. Secondary immigration (i.e. family reunification) has also been cut dramatically, from 50,000 in 1972 to around 11,500 in 1988. Nearly 54 per cent of the NCWP citizens granted settlement in 1988 were wives and children (see *Figure 2.1*).

In the Indian subcontinent, newly received applications for wives and children and other dependents fell from 24,680 in 1977 to 12,480 in 1986. In Bangladesh, demand also fell dramatically. In 1977 there were 15,200 newly received applications for entry made by wives and children and other persons. In 1986 the figure was 5,540.[9]

The 1971 Immigration Act stated that the rights of those already settled in the UK would not be adversely affected: for example, male Commonwealth citizens settled in Britain when the Act became law on 1 January 1973 had an automatic right to be joined here by their wives and children. The 1988 Immigration Act abolished this right. The third major migration phase, highlighted at the beginning of this section, is drawing to an end.[10]

2.9 Refugees and asylum seekers

In 1982 Britain granted full refugee status to 1,700 people (Gordon, 1989a, p. 5). Since 1987 the number of people seeking asylum has increased dramatically. People from Iran, Turkey, Somalia, Sri Lanka and Uganda account for most of the increase. In 1989 about 16,300 people were estimated to have applied for refugee status in the UK, three times the average for 1985–8 and ten times more than in 1979. Of these, 3,040 applications were granted. On 13 March 1991, in a written reply in the House of Commons, the Government revealed that the number of people applying to the UK for asylum nearly doubled in the previous year to 30,000 (see *Figure 2.2*).[11] It was expected to rise to 50,000 in 1991.[12] At the time of going to press the fate of Home Secretary Kenneth Baker's Asylum Bill was uncertain. The Bill, designed to isolate genuine asylum seekers from those the government claims are attempting to jump immigration queues, may become law during 1992. If it does, the number of refugees allowed to stay in Britain on humanitarian grounds could, on the government's own admission, be cut substantially (see *Independent*, 2 November 1991).

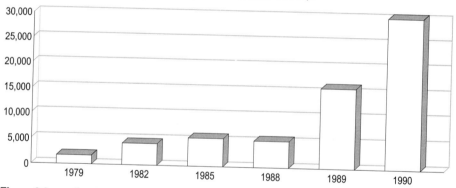

Figure 2.2: applications for refugee status in Great Britain
(*Adapted from the* Guardian, *3 July 1991*)

2.10 Illegal immigration, deportations and detentions

A corollary of restrictive immigration controls is the increasing importance attached to measures aimed at those already in Britain. Since 1979, the number of removals of illegal immigrants, deportations and detentions has increased.

Illegal immigration estimates vary. Of those people detected each year, approximately a half are Commonwealth citizens.[13] In 1979 deportations totalled 1,275. Between 1979 and 1987, 16,460 deportation orders were made, an average of 1,800 each year (Gordon, 1989a, p. 7), and 7,300 people were removed as illegal immigrants. In 1990, 4,280 people were removed from the UK either as illegal entrants or under the deportation process, a fall of 260 from 1989 (Home Office, 1991).

The use of immigration detention has also increased. The number of detainees – people held without trial in prisons and detention centres – reached 11,000, its highest ever level, in 1986. Under the 1988 Immigration Act, people who have not lived in Britain for seven years lost their right to appeal against deportation on compassionate grounds. The rights of Members of Parliament to intervene in immigrant issues – hitherto the most effective way of questioning the decisions of immigration officials – has also been severely restricted by government order (Gordon, 1989a, p. 10).

2.11 Entry for visitors

Before 1986 visitors from the Indian subcontinent, the Caribbean, and other Third World countries arriving in Britain without visas were checked through by immigration officers. Since 1986 short-stay visitors have required a six-month visa from British embassies and high commissions in their own countries. However, visitors from the USA and Australia, for example, do not have to obtain these short-stay visas. The Joint Council for the Welfare of Immigrants has claimed that this is indicative of racial bias. In 1990 the refusal rate for Guyanese visitors to Britain was 1 in 87, compared, for example, with 1 in 3,600 for Norwegians. A parliamentary reply in July 1989 revealed that Home and Foreign Office entry clearance officers at the British High Commission in New Delhi had rejected 5,350 out of the 42,410 (or 1 in 8) applications for visitors' visas (the corresponding figures were 1 in 4 for Bangladesh and 1 in 6 for Pakistan). There was a backlog of 21,800 unheard appeals from disappointed travellers by the end of 1989. The number of Jamaican visitors turned back at Heathrow almost tripled between 1987 and 1989. The Jamaican foreign minister told British ministers in October 1989 that the issue had caused 'a lot of ill feeling and tension', both on the island and in the Jamaican community in Britain.[14]

Notes

1 Letter of 22 June 1948 to the Labour Prime Minister, Clement Attlee, signed by eleven Labour MPs two days after the ship, the *Empire Windrush*, had brought 500 Afro-Caribbean migrants to the UK. Cited in Carter *et al.* (1987) p. 2.

2 Margaret Thatcher, 30 January 1978, in an interview on Granada Television quoted in Gordon (1989a).

3 Immigration policy since 1945 is analysed in J. Solomos, 'The politics of immigration since 1945' in Braham *et al.* (eds) (1992) (ED356 Reader 3).

4 Parliamentary Reports, 1905, cited in Coleman (1987) p. 1145. The figures used at this time were ten-yearly census data on 'aliens' domiciled in Britain: a set of data was published in 1901.

5 The IPS provides a sample of intending immigrants and emigrants of all nationalities and all origins and destinations (except the Republic of Ireland). A migrant is a person intending to stay in the UK for up to twelve months, having been outside the country for at least twelve months: and *vice versa* for an emigrant. Data are obtained on citizenship, country of previous residence and of birth, gender, age, marital status, previous occupation and UK destination. Response rate to the IPS is about 85 per cent.

6 Analysis by occupation and age of IPS data is usually published in coarse categories and is seldom cross-tabulated. New Commonwealth and Pakistani arrivals are not cross-tabulated by age and gender together.

7 See Devis (1985) pp. 13–20. Curiously enough, in the nineteenth century the preoccupation was with the control of emigration, not immigration.

8 See 1981 census, Country of Birth, Table 1, OPCS.

9 See S. Helm, 'Immigration: fears of a flood which has shrunk to a trickle', *Independent*, 4 December 1987.

10 The next major migration phases could be white migrants from South Africa and people from Hong Kong.

11 Quoted in the *Independent*, 'Question and answer: written replies', 13 March 1991.

12 *Independent*, 28 May 1991; *Guardian*, 3 July 1991.

13 The total includes overstayers as well as persons entering the UK illegally. See Coleman (1987) p. 1156.

14 See *Independent*, 9 November 1990.

3 RACIAL VIOLENCE AND HARASSMENT

▼ ▼

As a boy sleeps, a pig's head, its eyes, ears, nostrils and mouth stuffed with lighted cigarettes, is hurled through the window of his bedroom. A family do not leave their home after seven in the evening; they stay in one large room, having barricaded their ground floor. A family are held prisoner in their own flat by a security cage bolted to their front door by white neighbours. A youth is slashed with a knife by an older white boy as he walks along a school corridor between classes. A family home is burned out and a pregnant woman and her three children killed. A ticket collector is stabbed in the eye with a metal stake and killed simply because he refused to take racial abuse from some white passengers.

These cases, all reported in the last few years, are part of the black experience of Britain in the 1980s, part of black people's reality.

(Gordon, 1990, p. v)

▲ ▲

3.1 The context of racial violence and harassment

Racial violence and harassment are not recent phenomena. In 1919, there was a series of attacks on black people in the dock areas of Britain – Cardiff, Glasgow, Liverpool, Hull, Manchester and London. In the 1940s there were attacks in Liverpool (1948), Deptford (1949) and Birmingham (1949). In the late 1950s black people became a particular target for racist white youths. The 1960s brought 'paki-bashing' and attacks by white 'skinheads'. The 1970s saw racial violence and harassment escalate, culminating in *Blood on the Streets*, a report that illustrated the scale of violence suffered by the Bangladeshi community in the Spitalfields area of Tower Hamlets (Bethnal Green and Stepney Trades Council, 1978). The report raised concern and awareness about the intensity of the problem. Evidence suggests that the situation worsened in the 1980s. The Home Affairs Committee in its 1986 report, *Racial Attacks and Harassment*, accepted as its starting point that: 'the most shameful and dispiriting aspects of race relations in Britain is the incidence of racial attacks and harassment' (Home Affairs Committee, 1986, p. 22).[1]

The Runnymede Trust estimated that between January 1970 and November 1989, 74 people died as a result of attacks which were either known to be racially motivated because of evidence at subsequent trials, or widely believed to be so within the black community.[2]

Racial violence and harassment are not solely British problems. The EC has estimated that the number of racist attacks across the twelve community states rose by between 5 and 10 per cent in the late 1980s. The EC has called for a European Charter to protect its minority ethnic group population of 14 million, claiming that they will face increasing harassment, violence and discrimination unless member countries act to curb neo-facism, anti-semitism and organized racism.[3]

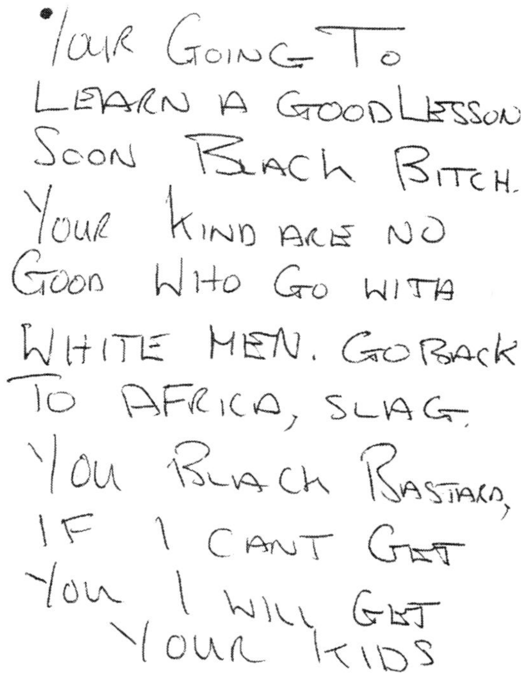
YOUR GOING TO
LEARN A GOOD LESSON
SOON BLACK BITCH.
YOUR KIND ARE NO
GOOD WHO GO WITH
WHITE MEN. GO BACK
TO AFRICA, SLAG.
YOU BLACK BASTARD,
IF I CANT GET
YOU I WILL GET
YOUR KIDS

***Figure 3.1:* hate mail pushed through the letterbox of a black family**
*(*Independent, *13 February 1990)*

3.2 Under-reporting of racial incidents

Assessing the incidence of racial harassment is difficult because incidents often go unreported. In 1989 a Home Affairs Select Committee highlighted a significant level of under-reporting of racial incidents revealed in Home Office and police evidence to the committee's inquiry.[4] The committee's chairman, Conservative MP John Wheeler, called racial harassment: 'a particularly disturbing, very horrifying crime … [which] affects not only individual victims but minority ethnic group communities as a whole. It engenders fear and militates against the creation of a decent and civilised multi-racial society.'[5]

In England and Wales, estimates based on incidents reported to the police suggest there are 7,000 racially motivated attacks each year.[6] The EC has argued that the real figure could be ten times higher, bringing the number of attacks to 70,000 (European Parliament, 1990, p. 68). Local studies in the UK have pointed to the low level of reporting. A London Borough of Newham (1987) report argued that the real level of racial attacks was about 20 times higher than the figures given by the police. In May 1991, a survey for Victim Support, backed by the Home Office, estimated that the number of incidents recorded by the police in England and Wales – between 3,000 and 6,000 – represented between 2 per cent and 5 per cent of the actual total. This study, of 700 cases over a two-year period in Camden, Southwark and Newham, also argued that, while cases that were reported were treated sympathetically at first, often 'nothing appeared to be done to arrest or charge the perpetrator' (Victim Support, 1991). In commenting on this report, a representative of the Community Involvement and Crime Prevention Branch of the Metropolitan Police questioned the narrowness of its sample and also offered an alternative and, he claimed, broader definition of what constitutes a racial incident: 'an occurrence where racial motivation is thought by the victim, the police, or any other person to be present' (*Independent*, 18 May 1991).

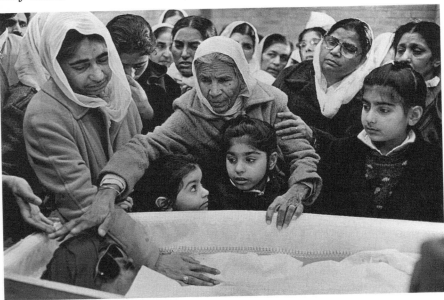

Figure 3.2: the funeral of murdered minicab driver Kuldip Sekhon. The dark glasses and turban hide multiple stab-wounds.

3.3 The extent of racial incidents

The number of racially motivated incidents in England and Wales during 1988, 1989 and 1990 were 4,383, 5,044 and 6,359 respectively. The available figures for Scotland for the same years were 299, 376 and 636.

(Runnymede Trust, 1991a, p. 7)

Provincial police forces and the Metropolitan Police, in evidence to the Home Affairs Committee, have reported an increase in the number of racial incidents. In 1984, 1,515 racial incidents were reported to the Metropolitan Police. By 1988 this had risen to 2,214. In the first six months of 1989, 1,290 incidents had been reported. Serious racial assaults recorded by the Metropolitan Police in the first half of 1989 rose by 60 per cent compared to 1988 (from 120 to 190). Official figures showed increases in racial incidents in six out of eight of London's police areas (*Guardian*, 14 August 1989). In his annual report for 1989, Metropolitan Police Commissioner, Sir Peter Imbert, identified a 22 per cent rise in 'racial incidents' and a 25 per cent rise in racially motivated assaults. He commented:

Racial attacks and any form of harassment on racial grounds are not only against the law they are also morally repugnant. Everyone has the right to feel safe at home and on the streets, but not all people do. Far too many are afraid of becoming victims of harassment or attack ... It is encouraging that more people are now willing to come forward and report these incidents but depressing that there are still those who are of such a bigoted nature that they indulge in such attacks. The clear-up rate for racial incidents in 1989 stood at just over 30% and we are determined to tackle this particular crime with increasing vigour.

(Metropolitan Police, 1990)

In June 1991, at a press conference introducing his 1990 annual report, Imbert reiterated his concern about the escalating number of reported racial incidents. In 1990 these rose by a further 8 per cent. He also reported that one officer had been disciplined in connection with racist behaviour in 1990, and one in the first half of 1991. Fewer than one in twelve complainants from minority ethnic groups had complained about an officer's racial attitudes. The force was often unable to prove complaints because of the standard of proof required at disciplinary hearings (*Independent*, 13 June 1991).

In the provinces, other research has confirmed the upward trend in racial incidents. According to a study in Leicester in 1987, many Asian families were living in a self-imposed curfew within their own homes because of the increase in attacks (Chambers Community Consultants, 1989). In Sheffield, a city council report concluded that all minorities were affected (Racial Harassment Project, 1989). Research in the first nine months of 1988 found that 25 per cent of incidents reported involved physical violence resulting in broken bones, facial injuries, loss of teeth and multiple bruising. All black people, male or female, rich or poor, were potential targets, irrespective of where they lived in the city. A quarter of the victims were under nineteen, as were the attackers. In 30 per cent of cases the attacker was actually known to the victim, either as a work colleague or a neighbour. Many Chinese people had come to see racial harassment as a condition of living in Britain: one told the research team it was 'almost as British as the weather'. Sheffield's Yemeni community complained of harassment at work, in the street, and in school.

The *1988 British Crime Survey*, which covered many crimes not reported to the police, showed Asians to be disproportionately more likely to be victims of crimes such as vandalism and victimization by groups of strangers that could not be accounted for by demographic or residential factors. The survey concluded that racism contributed to Asians becoming the victims of crime far more than it did with Afro-Caribbeans (Mayhew *et al.*, 1989).

Figure 3.3: room after a racist attack.

3.4 Racial incidents in people's homes

In 1987 the Commission for Racial Equality (CRE) published a report on racist incidents in people's homes (1987a). Based on a national sample of local authorities and agencies such as Community Relations Councils (CRCs), law centres and voluntary housing aid centres, it emphasized that the scale of the problem continues to go unreported. Over a third of the 142 local authorities that had policies on racial harassment considered the problem to be increasing. Among agencies surveyed, over 80 per cent thought racial harassment was an issue in their areas. By the end of the 1980s the situation had deteriorated, particularly in London where some boroughs were reporting a significant escalation in the number of reported racial attacks. For example, Southwark reported a 56 per cent rise between 1987 and 1989 (*Independent*, 13 February 1990). Section 7.7 of this book summarizes trends in housing department responses to racial harassment and violence, especially what courses of action can be taken against racist council tenants.

3.5 Racial incidents in educational institutions

In 1988 a major national report highlighted the pervasiveness of racial incidents in schools and colleges. *Learning in Terror* concluded: 'Racial harassment is widespread and persistent – and in most areas very little is done about it'.[7] The report found that the problem increasingly affected all the education system, and encompassed the lives of pupils and students, staff and parents. They found it a feature of largely white schools in rural and suburban Britain as well as schools in the inner cities. Of the 115 educational institutions surveyed, only 47 had published or were working on guidelines to combat racial harassment.[8]

3.6 Inter-ethnic group conflict

There have been reports of some tension between young members of ethnic communities living in the Tower Hamlets area of London. For example, it was reported that despite great efforts by Bengali elders and community workers, the pressures of recession and poverty had led to clashes between young Bangladeshis and young Somalis who had arrived since the war of 1988. But the Capa Organisation, a voluntary group which monitors police activity in Tower Hamlets, has claimed that among the causes of tension between young Bengalis and Somalis are the absence of facilities for the

Somali community (unlike the Bengalis they had no youth centre) and police harassment of the Asian community in general. Tim Kelsey reported the creation of small vigilante groups of young Bengalis watching out for the police (Tim Kelsey, *Independent on Sunday*, 26 May 1991).

Notes

1   Evidence for the mounting scale of racial harassment was presented in CRE (1981); Home Office (1981); GLC (1984); Runnymede Trust (1986).

2   See Gordon (1990) pp. 8 and 43. This should not be taken as the maximum total. Other attacks may well have gone unreported.

3   See European Parliament (1990) p. 68; BBC Radio 4, *Special Assignment*, 'Racism in Europe', 11 July 1990; *Guardian*, 15 October 1990; and MEP Mr G. Ford's letter to the *Guardian*, 17 October 1990.

4   Home Affairs Select Committee (1989). Police forces in England and Wales have been required to collect statistics on racial incidents since 1986, and in Scotland since 1987.

5   At the press conference to launch the report and quoted in the *Independent*, 21 December 1989.

6   In June 1991, Peter Lloyd, Parliamentary Under Secretary of State at the Home Office, was reported as telling the House of Commons that 6,459 racially motivated attacks were reported to the police in England and Wales in 1990/1 (*Independent*, 9 June 1991). See also Mayhew *et al.* (1989) and Gordon (1989b).

7   A. Hayes, CRE Chief Executive in his foreword to CRE (1988a) p. 5. The report was based on a national LEA monitoring exercise in 1987 in England, Scotland and Wales. See also Gordon (1990) pp. 14–15 for a list of media reports on racial violence and harassment in schools and on young people on their way to and from school, or outside school.

8   For a fuller discussion of racial incidents in schools see Troyna and Hatcher (1992) (Open University course ED356 Reader 1).

4 'RACE', INEQUALITY AND POVERTY

▼ ▼

Blackness and poverty are more correlated than they were some years ago. In spite of government concern with racial disadvantage, and the undoubted limited success of positive action and equal opportunities in helping to create a black middle class, the condition of the black poor is deteriorating.

(Amin and Leech, cited in Oppenheim, 1990, p. 79).[1]

Officially, poverty does not exist in Britain. The government does not define a 'poverty line'. It argues that an objective definition is impossible, that any attempt to count the poor is doomed because it will depend on the subjective judgements of experts about what it is to be poor.

(Frayman, 1991a, p. 2)

▲ ▲

4.1 Poverty and inequality: the general context

In the autumn of 1990 the Child Poverty Action Group (CPAG) estimated that ten and a half million people – 18.5 per cent of Britain's population, including three million children – were living in poverty.[2] The scale of the problem was confirmed by the Market and Opinion Research Institute (MORI) survey for the 1991 television series *Breadline Britain 1990s* (see *Figure 4.1*).

In December 1990 research conducted for the United Nations International Children's Emergency Fund (UNICEF) and the National Children's Bureau by Professor Jonathan Bradshaw of York University reinforced CPAG findings. Between 1979 and 1987 the number of children whose families earned less than half of the average income increased from 1,620,000 to 3,090,000 – a rise from 12 per cent to 26 per cent of all children.[3]

In 1990 the CPAG concluded that Britain had begun to witness a reversal of a long-term trend: the share of income of the poorer sections of UK society shrank in the 1980s (Oppenheim, 1990, pp. 24–44).[4] According to figures released by the Department of Social Security (DSS) in July 1990, income inequality widened between 1979 and 1988, becoming greater than at any time since the Second World War (Oppenheim, 1990, p. 35; Atkinson, 1990). *Figures 4.2* and *4.3*, analysing DSS figures, confirm the *Breadline Britain* survey findings: more children were living in poorer families and the incomes of the poorest increased the least (DSS, 1990).[5]

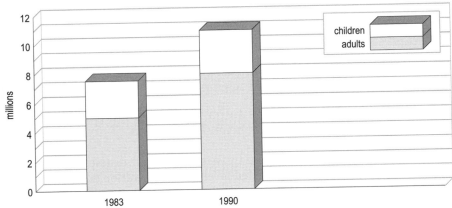

Figure 4.1: numbers in poverty in Great Britain
(Adapted from Frayman, 1991a, p. 9)

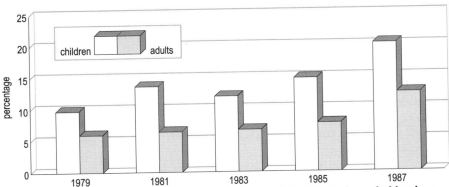

Figure 4.2: percentage of children and adults in Great Britain living in households where income is less than half the national average
(Adapted from the Independent on Sunday, *29 July 1990)*

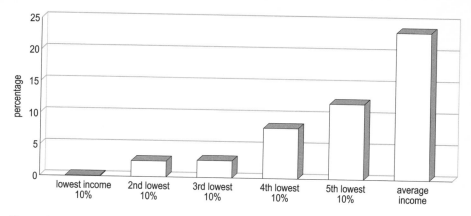

Figure 4.3: percentage increase in real income in Great Britain (discounting inflation), 1978–87, for people in the bottom half of the income distribution
(Adapted from the Independent on Sunday, 29 July 1990)

Other research confirmed the relative impoverishment of the poor:

- In March 1991 research by Peter Townsend, Professor of Social Policy at Bristol University, showed that the incomes of the poorest 20 per cent of the population fell by just under 5 per cent between 1979 and 1989 while the income of the richest percentile increased by 40 per cent (Townsend, 1991).[6]

- In April 1991 the EC found that between 1980 and 1985 the increase in the number of people living in poverty – from 8.2 million to 10.3 million – was greater in the UK than in any other EC country. One in five of all EC residents defined by the EC as poor lives in the UK (*Independent*, 17 May 1991; *Guardian*, 8 April 1991).

- In May 1991 a House of Commons committee estimated that between 1979 and 1988 the number of people with incomes below half the national average grew by 3.7 million to 9.1 million (Social Security Committee, 1991).

- In October 1991 the CPAG reported that 11.8 million people lived in poverty, more than double the figure in 1978 (*Guardian*, 23 October 1991; CPAG, 1991).

Figures 4.4 and *4.5* show the risk of poverty by economic and family status in 1987. Of all single parents – whether in or out of work – nearly half were living in poverty. Children at greatest risk lived in families where there was unemployment (nearly 8 children out of every 10 in unemployed families lived in poverty) or where there was a single parent (6 children in every 10 in single-parent families lived in poverty). In 1987, 1.1 million children living in poverty were found in lone-parent families – 45 per cent of *all* children in poverty. Seventy per cent of children in lone-parent families were living in poverty compared to 13 per cent in two-parent families (Oppenheim, 1990, pp. 29–33).

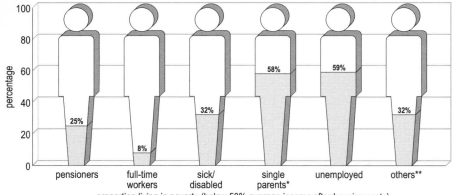

* single parents who are not in full-time work
** men aged 60-4, widows, students, people temporarily away from work, carers, people who are unemployed but not available for work

Figure 4.4: risk of poverty in Great Britain by economic status, 1987
(Adapted from Oppenheim, 1990, p. 30)

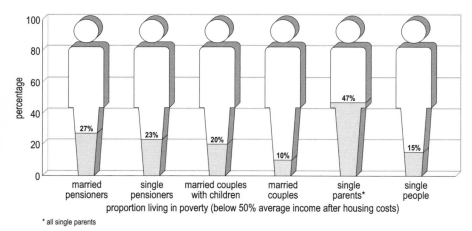

* all single parents

Figure 4.5: risk of poverty in Great Britain by family status, 1987
(Adapted from Oppenheim, 1990, p. 30)

Figure 4.6 shows the groups most at risk from poverty. The television series *Breadline Britain in the 1990s* found that the two groups most at risk were the unemployed and single parents (Frayman, 1991a, p. 10). *Figures 4.7* and *4.8*, based on data from the *Family Expenditure Survey* and other government statistics, show the extent to which the skilled members of British society have gained relatively more than the poor during the 1980s.[7]

In September 1990 the government's *New Earnings Survey* showed that the gap between high- and low-paid employees was wider than at any time since records began in 1886 (Department of Employment, 1990a). Between 1979 and 1987, the poorest 10 per cent of the population saw their incomes grow in real terms by 0.1 per cent after housing costs, whilst the average income rose in real terms by 23 per cent (Oppenheim, 1990, p. 44). In 1987, 70 per cent of the income of the poorest 10 per cent came from social security benefits compared with 17 per cent for the population as a whole (Oppenheim, 1990, pp. 34–6). During the 1980s, 1 million households – involving 3 million people – were registered as homeless, while another million were refused registration.[8]

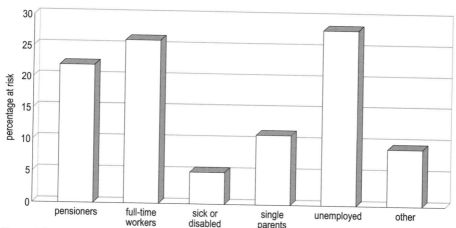

Figure 4.6: percentage of the population in Great Britain in poverty by vulnerable group, 1987 *(Adapted from Oppenheim, 1990, p. 30)*

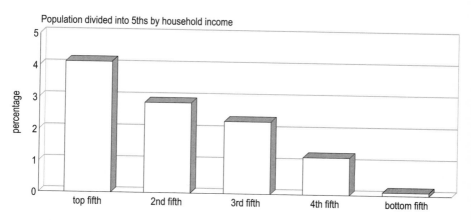

Figure 4.7: real income growth per year in Great Britain, 1977–90

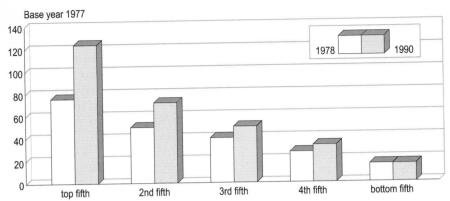

Figure 4.8: real personal disposable income in Great Britain in £millions: population divided into fifths by household income

Child benefit contributes 11 per cent to the incomes of the poorest 10 per cent. It was frozen between 1987 and 1991. During the 1980s, CPAG estimated that while tax allowances had increased in real terms by 25 per cent, the value of child benefit dropped by 8 per cent.[9] The unfreezing of child benefit in the March budget of 1991 did little to recover this real loss of benefit.

In July 1991 the DSS revealed that, in 1990, 27,000 people were refused loans from the Social Fund, the government's safety net for the poor, because they were too poor to repay the loan.[10]

4.2 'Race', poverty and the labour market

Very little empirical work exists *specifically* about 'race' and poverty.[11] The DSS's *Households Below Average Income* and *Low Income Families*, the official data sources for estimating poverty levels in Britain, include no breakdown by 'race' in relation to several indicators which, as our general analysis suggests, are key factors in any measure of poverty.

Between 1987 and 1989 the Labour Force Surveys (LFS) figures showed that the male unemployment rate for minority ethnic groups was 14 per cent, compared with 9 per cent for white people. Thirteen per cent of women in minority ethnic groups were unemployed, compared to 8 per cent of white women (see also Section 10.6) (DoE, 1991).

The young are especially affected. During the same period, 25 per cent of Afro-Caribbean, 16 per cent of Indian and 27 per cent of Pakistani or Bangladeshi young people aged between 16 and 24 were unemployed, compared to 12 per cent of white people (Oppenheim, 1990, p.79–80).

When in employment, black people tend to be located in low-pay industries, often involving shift work or intermittent, cyclical work (DoE, 1990b). Black people still tend to work in the manufacturing and manual work for which they were first recruited in the 1950s and 1960s, their job status shaped by immigration policy and vulnerable to recession.[12]

In 1982 the third Policy Studies Institute (PSI) survey revealed that West Indian and Asian men earned less than white men: PSI found that white women earned more than Asian women, but less than West Indian women (Brown, 1984, p. 214).

Table 4.1: weekly earned income for each household member in the 1982 PSI survey: studied groups compared by household type

	Extended households	Lone parents	Others with children	Adults without children
White	£46	£20	£37	£59
West Indian	£37	£24	£32	£51
Asian	£27	£21	£27	£50

(Brown, 1984, p. 231)

Table 4.1 compares the weekly earned income for each household member in the PSI survey in relation to dependency ratios. In extended households and in nuclear families the earned income per person is lower among West Indians than among whites, but is particularly low among Asians.

In 1988, 53 per cent of men from minority ethnic groups were employed in the distribution, hotels and catering sectors where wages are low, compared to 36 per cent of white men (DoE, 1990b). LFS data showed that in the same year 55 per cent of men from minority ethnic groups worked in industries where 30 per cent or more of the workforce earned below £130 per week, compared to 33 per cent of white men.[13] Residential location and segregation also predisposes black people towards unemployment and low pay. At the time of the third PSI survey, 70 per cent of Asians and 81 per cent of Afro-Caribbeans lived in the former metropolitan county areas, mostly in inner city locations, compared with only 31 per cent of white people (Brown, 1984, pp. 54–67). The industrial retreat from the city heartlands during the recession of the early 1980s had a disproportionate effect on opportunities for black people.

4.3 Are black people more at risk?

No government statistics provide breakdowns of benefit claimants by ethnic origin. The third PSI survey found that 34 per cent of white households claimed child benefit compared to 60 per cent of West Indian and 75 per cent of Asian households. Asian extended households were far more reliant on child benefit than white and West Indian households (Brown, 1984, p. 242).

Black people are less likely than white people to claim benefits to which they are entitled. The data are therefore likely to underestimate the number of black people eligible for benefits (see Section 5 on health and Section 6 on social services and welfare benefits).

> Fear of creating problems, concern that any fuss might affect residence, the lack of translated information, and no recognition by the DSS of any responsibility to provide interpreters, have all created a climate in which black citizens are less likely to assert their rights, doubting their entitlement to benefits.
>
> (Oppenheim, 1990, p. 89)

Official data sources fail also to measure the extent to which immigration policy has forced some black people *outside* the welfare net. The 1971 Immigration Act, for example, introduced a rule allowing wives and children of Commonwealth citizens into the UK only if a sponsor could support and accommodate them without recourse to 'public funds'. 'Public funds' – clearly defined in 1985 for the first time – referred to housing benefit, family income supplement (now family credit), supplementary benefit (now income support), and housing under Part III of the Housing Act, 1985. Some black people have thus suffered hardship in the struggle to settle in the UK without help from the state. The extension of means-tested benefits under 1988 social security legislation further exacerbated the situation (for example, questions on the date of arrival in the UK have been added to the income support claimant form).

Table 4.2 illustrates how residence conditions can impact on 'race' and poverty by limiting welfare options (Oppenheim, 1990, pp. 84; 89-90). For example, in order to claim child benefit, the claimant must have been in the UK for six months.

Oppenheim's survey also reveals:

- the age profile of black people is younger than whites, making black people more susceptible to freezes in child benefits and cuts in income support;
- Afro-Caribbean families are over three times more likely than white families to be lone-parent families. Lone-parent families are particularly vulnerable to poverty, low pay for women and expensive child-care provision tending to keep lone parents on benefit (Oppenheim, 1990, p. 86).

Table 4.2: residence conditions for some non-contributory benefits

Child benefit
Present in UK for 6 months

Severe disablement allowance
Residence in the UK for 10 out of the previous 20 years

Invalid care allowance, attendance allowance
Residence in the UK for 26 weeks in the previous 52 weeks

Mobility allowance
Residence in the UK for 52 weeks in the previous 18 months

Non-contributory widows benefit and category C retirement pension
Resident for 10 years in the period 5 July 1948 to 1 November 1970 or date of claim

Category D retirement pension
Resident in the UK for 10 years in the previous 20 years

Note: In addition to a residence test, people generally have to have been in Britain for a period of 6 months before claiming.
(Oppenheim, 1990, p. 90)

Extended families are also more vulnerable. PSI found that 17 per cent of West Indian people and 22 per cent of Asian people lived in households with more than three adults, compared with 6 per cent of white people (Brown, 1984, p. 45; see also Section 1 on demographic trends).

Changes in taxation can also have a disproportionate effect on black households, especially large ones. For example, at the time of the introduction of the Community Charge, 75 per cent of families with three adults or more were estimated by the government to lose out compared to only 25 per cent who gained.[14]

Oppenheim concludes:

> Every indicator of poverty shows that black people and other ethnic minority groups are more at risk of high unemployment, low pay, shift work and poor social security rights. Their poverty is caused by immigration policies which have often excluded people from abroad from access to welfare, employment patterns which have marginalised black people and other ethnic groups into low paid manual work, direct and indirect discrimination in social security and the broader experience of racism in society as a whole.

(Oppenheim, 1990, p. 91)

Notes

1   Readers should note that this section is particularly related to the sections on demographic trends, immigration, health, welfare and the labour market.

2   What is poverty? In their 1990 analysis, CPAG used the two most commonly accepted definitions: (a) people on 50 per cent of average income, (b) people with incomes at supplementary benefit level. In addition, CPAG took account of people living just above each of these poverty lines. CPAG described anyone living on between 100 and 140 per cent of supplementary benefit or between 50 and 60 per cent of average income as living on 'the margins of poverty' (Oppenheim, 1990, p. 18). The 10.5 million figure relates to (a) above – the official EC poverty line – and was arrived at after deducting for housing costs (see Atkinson, 1990). See also Frayman (1991a) where the definition of poverty was based on people lacking 'life necessities' (e.g. domestic heating, essential clothing, two meals a day, savings, etc.) For a fuller analysis of CPAG's findings see Frayman (1991b).

3   See Bradshaw (1990). The television series *Breadline Britain*, transmitted in 1991 by London Weekend Television, revealed that 11 million people in Britain were living in poverty. The series' previous survey, in 1983, showed 3.5 million to be living in poverty.

    Note that the statistics referred to here are snapshots – they do not show the length of time people are living in poverty. The people living on or below supplementary benefit or 50 per cent of average income in 1987 may be different people from those living on those levels in 1979.

4   We are greatly indebted to Carey Oppenheim's invaluable work which has framed much of this analysis.

5   Reproduced in *Independent on Sunday*, 19 July 1990.

6   This was the first publication of a unit established because of concern about the use of statistics by government. See also Statistical Monitoring Unit (1991).

7   Figures 4.7 and 4.8 are drawn from P. Ormerod and E. Salama, 'The rise of the British underclass', *Independent*, 19 June 1990.

8   See Malcolm Dean, 'The poor state of Major's nation', *Guardian*, 5 December 1990.

9   See DSS (1990) table G1 and annex 1 table G1. See also *Independent*, 29 October 1988.

10   See *Independent*, 18 July 1991.

11   DSS (1990; 1988). A wealth of official statistical sources on poverty were lost during the 1980s. For example, the Royal Commission on Income and Wealth and the Supplementary Benefit Commission, which regularly published information, were abolished.

12   See Brown (1984) pp. 185–227. The *New Earnings Survey*, Department of Employment, does not provide breakdowns by 'race' or ethnic origin. Much of what we know about 'race' and income is reliant on independent research. See, for example, West Midlands Low Pay Unit (1988).

13   See Oppenheim (1990) p. 81. The figures combine data from the *New Earnings Survey*, 1988 (DoE, 1989) with the LFS.

14   Department of Employment press release, 15 February 1988, Table 10.

5 'RACE' AND HEALTH

> It is clear that the ... services of Britain have been slow to accommodate to the changing needs of an increasing multi-ethnic and multicultural society. Many of the 'problems' and needs identified 10 or 20 years ago are still key issues awaiting resolution ... there is still a long way to go before the 'caring institutions' can be said to care equally for all irrespective of racial or ethnic origins – and in the meanwhile all the pressure that can be brought to bear is required.

(Johnson, 1987, p. 133)

5.1 'Race' and health data

The general problem of data availability is particularly acute in the area of inequality in health and the health service:

> Another important dimension to inequality in contemporary Britain is race. Immigrants to this country from the so-called New Commonwealth, whose ethnic identity is clearly visible in the colour of their skin, are known to experience greater difficulties finding work and adequate housing ... Given these disabilities it is to be expected that they might also record rather higher than average rates of mortality and morbidity. This hypothesis is difficult to test from official statistics, since 'race' has rarely been assessed in official censuses and surveys.

(Townsend and Davidson, 1982, p. 58)

5.2 'Race', morbidity and mortality

Section 4 traced the links between 'race' and poverty, particularly in childhood. The 1990 Child Poverty Action Group (CPAG) survey also revealed the significant relationship which exists between material deprivation and ill health (Oppenheim, 1990, pp. 58-61). Research into poor health and premature death has long pointed to the deleterious effect that adverse socio-economic conditions have on the health of children of all ages: more recently evidence of differential health related to 'race' has emerged (see, for example, Townsend and Davidson, 1982, p. 58; Whitehead, 1987). In 1990 a study of 593 children admitted to an East London hospital – mostly suffering from respiratory tract infections and gastroenteritis – found that minority ethnic group children were disproportionately represented: 48 per cent came from families whose head of household was Asian, African or Caribbean, though these groups accounted for only 18 per cent of the population in Hackney and 11 per cent in Tower Hamlets. The authors concluded that good health was more likely to be facilitated by improving housing conditions and ameliorating poverty than by improving hospital and medical services (Carter *et al.*, 1990). The *British Medical Journal*, reappraising the Black Report ten years on, reaffirmed the strong relationships that exist between health and class divisions in British society: it concluded that the evidence from studies of differential mortality 'reiterates the fact that British society is stratified to a fine grain from top to bottom' (Davy Smith *et al.*, 1990).

Office of Population Services and Censuses (OPCS) figures examining infant mortality by mother's country of birth from 1982 to 1985 show that while mortality for immigrant mothers from India, Bangladesh and East Africa corresponds to the indigenous-born population, the infant mortality rate for children born to mothers from Pakistan and the Caribbean is considerably higher (see *Figure 5.1*).

All immigrant groups showed excess perinatal and neonatal mortality over the indigenous population, but after the first month of life mortality was only raised for Caribbeans and Pakistanis. Caribbeans and Pakistanis were thus the only immigrant groups to reveal excess mortality throughout infancy (Britton, 1989, pp. 21–2). Looking at infant mortality trends from 1975 to 1984, the Radical Statistics Race Group (RSRG) study observed that:

- rates have been consistently higher for mothers born in the New Commonwealth and Pakistan (NCWP) than for those born in the UK;

- rates were falling faster for mothers born in the UK than for mothers born in the NCWP;

- mothers born in India and Bangladesh revealed a considerable recent reduction in rates.

From this they concluded that there are 'considerable disparities in health experience between white and black populations as a whole at and around childbirth' (Bhat *et al.*, 1988, pp. 180–1).

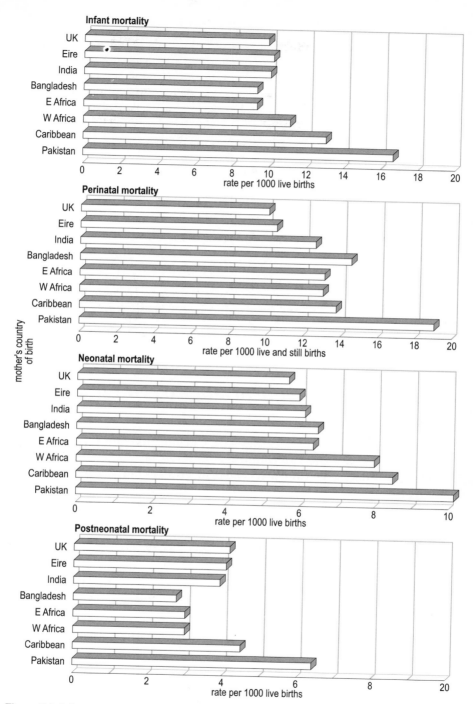

Figure 5.1: infant, perinatal, neonatal and postneonatal mortality rates by mother's country of birth, 1982–5, England and Wales
(Adapted from Britton, 1989, p. 21)

Britton's study for the OPCS in 1989 concluded:

> Throughout infancy Asian infants, and Pakistanis in particular, showed raised mortality from *congenital anomalies*. This was combined with higher levels of mortality from *perinatal conditions* in the perinatal period. On the other hand *sudden infant deaths* and deaths from *respiratory diseases* occurred at a lower rate for most Asian infants. For West African and Caribbean infants congenital anomalies were not the major causes of death; instead they experienced relatively high mortality throughout infancy from perinatal conditions. The Caribbeans had a rate of sudden infant death roughly similar to the level for the UK group.

> (Britton, 1989, p. 22)

Research has highlighted other differences surrounding childbirth. For example, maternal mortality rates are relatively higher among those women born in Africa, the Caribbean and the Indian subcontinent. Department of Health and Social Security (DHSS) findings published in 1982 into maternal deaths in England and Wales for the periods 1970–2, 1973–5, and 1976–8 show maternal death rates from obstetric causes to be 0.32 per 1,000 live births for women born in NCWP compared with 0.11 for other women.[1]

5.3 Ill-health specific to minority ethnic groups

Sickle cell disease (mainly affecting Afro-Caribbeans) and rickets (mostly affecting Asians) are the two conditions differentially affecting the black British population which have received most attention.[2] Other work has pointed to:

- birthweight differentials between the white and black populations;

- anaemias other than sickle cell;

- tuberculosis, now of rising concern among the homeless (see Section 7.6);

- health problems caused by the long-acting contraceptive Depo-provera, disproportionately prescribed to black women;

- the low take-up of antenatal and postnatal care services by black people (see Community Relations Commission, 1977; Torkington, 1983; Darbyshire, 1983).

5.4 Mental health: admissions, diagnosis and treatment

The relationship between 'race' and mental health is an issue of increasing concern to black people and to some psychiatrists in Britain.

In 1989 an article in *Psychiatry Bulletin* argued that the question of 'race' was not simply another discrete demographic factor that could be understood within a medical theory of cause and effect, but one that touched on and reawakened doubts about psychiatry's function and role within society (Frances *et al.*, 1989, p. 482).

The reasons for this anxiety have a long history.[3] Measures used to indicate the psychiatric state of Britain's black population are problematic. Statistical evidence is disparate. National Health Service (NHS) and official statistics, such as the Hospital In-Patient Mental Health Inquiry, do not give data on ethnic origin. Moreover, many of the early independent research studies tended to rely on country of birth as a measure of ethnicity, and thus were unable to identify British-born black people.[4] This early evidence suggested, once age and gender factors had been taken into account, that admission rates for Afro-Caribbean-born males and females were significantly higher than for the British born population, and that admission rates for Indian, African, and Pakistani women may also be greater than for other women (Dean *et al.* 1981; Hitch, 1981).

Once admitted to hospital, black people appear to experience different diagnoses from whites. Cochrane found that Afro-Caribbeans were far more likely to be diagnosed as schizophrenic, the rate per 100,000 being 290 compared to 87 for those born in England and Wales (Cochrane, 1977). Dean *et al.* (1981) argued that, once age differences had been taken into account, Indian males were three times more likely to be diagnosed as schizophrenic, and Afro-Caribbean males and females five times more likely to be so diagnosed than UK-born first admissions.

Further research by Littlewood and Lipsedge (1987), in a six-year study in inner London, showed that people born in Britain to Afro-Caribbean parents were three times as likely to be admitted to hospital as diagnosed schizophrenics as other black people, and 12 times more likely than white Britons. In a 1989 BBC Horizon documentary, Glynn Harrison, a Nottingham psychiatrist, reported that the rate of diagnosed schizophrenia was 16 times higher for British-born blacks aged 16–19 than for British-born whites in the same age cohort.[5] Two reviews of the evidence collected in the 1960s and 1970s concluded that mental illness among minority ethnic groups revealed more diagnosed psychosis, but an under-representation of psychoneuroses and non-psychotic disorders (Ineichen, 1980; Rack, 1982).

Ineichen's research in four inner-city wards in Bristol illustrated how black people, especially Afro-Caribbeans, were more likely to come to hospital on a compulsory admission (Ineichen et al., 1984, pp. 600–11; Ineichen, 1986). Looking at Bradford first-time admissions, Hitch and Clegg (1980) found that across all admissions, people born in the New Commonwealth were up to four times more likely than white patients to reach hospital on the basis of police or social worker referral.

Rwgellera's research in London reported that significantly fewer black patients were referred by a General Practitioner than 'English' ones (Rwgellera, 1977, pp. 317–29; 1980, pp. 428–32). Pinto (1970), looking at admissions under the 1959 Mental Health Act, argued that black patients were twice as likely as white patients to be admitted under Section 136, and twice as likely as whites to have been admitted to hospital from prison – a finding substantiated by the research of Littlewood and Lipsedge (1982). In a three-year study of police referrals under Section 136 of the Mental Health (Amendment) Act 1983, MIND reported a disproportionate number of Afro-Caribbeans among all police referrals, and criticized the police for displaying 'inherent racism'.[6] Lipsedge argued that a black person diagnosed as mentally ill and arrested by the police was far more likely than a white counterpart to be imprisoned rather than admitted to hospital.[7] A study in Birmingham estimated that young people born in Britain to West Indian parents were 25 times more likely to be placed by courts into psychiatric care than their white counterparts. The researchers also claimed that British-born black women were 13 times more likely to be diagnosed as schizophrenic than white women.[8]

Research into psychiatric treatment suggests black people tend to receive harsher forms of medication than equivalent white groups (Littlewood and Cross, 1980, pp. 194–201; Bolton, 1984, pp. 77–84). During the mid-1980s, Rosemarie Cope found that Afro-Caribbeans are more likely to receive treatment in secure facilities (Cope, 1989, pp. 343–5). Moreover, black patients are more likely to receive electro-convulsive therapy (ECT) treatments than whites. Littlewood and Cross's research in an East London hospital found that the majority of patients given ECT were diagnosed as depressives, but that 39 per cent of black patients receiving ECT had not been diagnosed as depressed, compared to only 16 per cent of white patients receiving ECT. The administration of anti-depressant drugs to black women in particular (especially Afro-Caribbeans) has also been a recurring feature in mental health research and 'race' (Littlewood and Cross, 1980, pp. 194–201; Bryan et al. 1985).

5.5 Racial inequalities in the NHS: doctors, nurses and ancillary staff

During the 1980s research pointed to racial inequalities in NHS employment patterns, from consultant doctors to ancillary workers. Yasmin Alibhai revealed that in 1988 there were then only two Caribbean psychiatrists working in British mental hospitals (Alibhai, 1988, pp. 2–3). In 1980 a Policy Studies Institute (PSI) survey of 2,000 doctors found that 45 per cent of UK-born doctors were consultants, compared to only 9 per cent of Asian-born doctors (Smith, 1980). In 1985 DHSS figures showed that while overseas-born doctors formed 28 per cent of all hospital doctors, they were confined to the lower professional ranks. Where they had reached a higher job status, they were confined to the less popular branches of the profession (DHSS, 1986). In 1987, in a study which extended PSI analysis to British-born black doctors and overseas-born doctors trained in Britain, the Commission for Racial Equality (CRE) reported that racial inequalities among NHS doctors still confined minority ethnic group doctors to less popular and low status jobs, for example, in geriatrics and psychiatry. Doctors from minority ethnic groups suffered from poor training, lower promotion prospects and low pay. The research also showed that among doctors born overseas, nearly a third had to make more than ten applications before getting a job. The CRE study also reported that half of 'non-white' doctors and 40 per cent of their white colleagues believed there was racial discrimination in the NHS (CRE, 1987b). The then chair of the CRE, Sir Peter Newsam, observed:

> The commission is particularly concerned about the similar trend which seems to be developing among wholly British trained ethnic minority doctors. The research gives no ground for believing that this group will escape the discrimination that overseas doctors have experienced.

> (*Guardian*, 29 January 1987)

Discrimination also extended to selection for medical education. In February 1988 the CRE's formal investigation into St George's Hospital Medical School found that the school had directly discriminated on racial grounds, contrary to the Race Relations Act 1976, through the operation of its admissions computer program and in its candidate selection process (CRE, 1988d).[9]

Nurses are the largest category of NHS employees. A study of overseas nurses in Britain in 1971 showed that one in ten NHS hospital nurses were 'immigrant' and that 'immigrants' formed 20 per cent of pupil nurses, 15 per cent of midwives, and 14 per cent of student nurses. 'Immigrants' were, however, under-represented in senior nursing career grades (Thomas and Williams, 1972).[10] Minority ethnic group nurses, like doctors, are more likely to be found in particular specialities, such as geriatrics and mental health and other less popular career grades, for which lower academic standards have been set. Hicks' (1982) study for the *Nursing Times* found that overseas recruits were pressured into State Enrolled Nurse (SEN) rather than the higher status State Registered Nurse (SRN) training, and that black nurses encountered promotion difficulties.

Black people are also concentrated in NHS ancillary jobs, for example, in domestic, catering and cleaning and maintenance services. Doyal *et al.*'s (1980) study of migrant workers in a London hospital found that 78 per cent of its ancillary and maintenance staff were born overseas. In 1983 the CRE commented:

> the hospital service is as vulnerable to unlawful racial discrimination as other employing groups and specific cases of discrimination have taken place. Nevertheless, employing authorities do not seem to realise that racial discrimination can still take place in organisations which employ substantial numbers of ethnic minority staff.

(CRE, 1983b, pp. 14–5)

Despite progress since then, the report of the Equal Opportunities Task Force 1986–90, published in March 1991, pointed to 'glaring' racial inequalities in the NHS and called on the NHS to implement equal opportunity policies. The task force found that while most health authorities had set up equal opportunity policies, relatively few had translated their policies into a timetabled programme for action, or had allocated responsibilities or sufficient resources. Most had failed to produce data about the ethnic composition of their workforce or monitored the outcome of selection decisions, especially in regard to promotion procedures and outcomes. Few health authorities complied with the recommendations of the CRE code of practice, while equal opportunities had not yet become part of the formal and routine duties of health service managers. The report concluded that action was needed immediately even to maintain the limited progress made during the 1980s, but that the new market-style NHS, effective from April 1991, could not alone be relied upon as the means of achieving racial equality in the NHS.[11]

Notes

1   'Report on confidential enquiries into maternal deaths in England and Wales', Reports on Health and Social Subjects, DHSS, 1982, quoted in Bhat *et al.* (1988) p. 179.

2   See Tuck (1982); Anionwu *et al.* (1981) p. 283; Goel *et al.* (1976) p. 1141. It is important to note that progress has been made in relation to treatment. For example, in Scotland, particularly the Glasgow area, the incidence of rickets was substantially reduced by the health authorities providing calcium to all Asian parents.

3   For an excellent review of 'race' and mental health see Bhat *et al.* (1988) pp. 194–22. Much of the evidence presented here is taken from their research review. On the shortcomings of official health statistics see Doyal (1979) p. 243.

4   It is important to recognize that what is at issue in much of the data specific to Section 6 is the supposed 'neutrality' of clinical diagnosis. There is evidence which shows that clinical diagnosis in psychiatry is culturally specific. See, for example, Kubie (1971). Research has extended this analysis to linking the relationships between racism and diagnosis, particularly of schizophrenics. See, for example, Cochrane (1977); Carpenter and Brockington (1980); Dean *et al.* (1981); Hitch (1981).

5   BBC 1 *Horizon, Black Schizophrenia*, transmitted on 13 March 1989. The figures quoted in Harrison's research for Afro-Caribbeans may be distorted by misdiagnosis and double counting, by the small numer of cases studied by Harrison, by poor statistics on the numbers of British blacks, and by relative under-counting of white schizophrenics.

6   See Rogers and Faulkner (1987). There is also disturbing evidence of the mentally ill increasingly being imprisoned. The year ending 31 March 1990 saw a 38 per cent increase in the number of inmates referred to psychiatrists, from 12,285 to 16,937. No ethnically classified data is available on this population.

7   See 'Racism "may be the cause of mental illness in blacks"', *Independent*, 25 January 1990.

8   See 'Mental health study raps "racist" police', *Observer*, 1 January 1987.

9   The St George's Report illustrates the way in which 'liberal' institutions that appear to have a good track record on admissions and training with regards to minority ethnic groups can themselves operate systems which are discriminatory.

10 We have not documented gender differences here, though these are very marked in the NHS.

11 'The work of the Equal Opportunities Task Force 1986–1990: a final report', March 1991, King Edward's Hospital Fund for London, 14 Palace Court, London.

6 'RACE', SOCIAL SERVICES AND WELFARE BENEFITS

▼ ▼

In 1985, an HMSO report summarised the findings of nine DHSS funded studies in a report entitled 'Social Work Decisions in Child Care'. These studies explored the various aspects of the care career process ... It is pertinent to point out that not one of these nine studies focused on the 'race' dimension. This is perhaps also a reflection of the 'colour blind' approach which continues to exist in the personal social services.

(Barn, 1990, p. 229)

▲ ▲

6.1 Social services departments and equal opportunity policies

In 1989 a Commission for Racial Equality (CRE) survey showed that, while limited progress had been made in social services provision, few social services departments appeared to be taking race equality issues any more seriously than they did in 1979. Even among those departments which had committed themselves to promoting equality of opportunity, policy implementation was still embryonic. The CRE concluded that most social service departments were not meeting their duties under Section 71 of the Race Relations Act 1976 – the section requiring local authorities to take steps to tackle racial discrimination and promote equality of opportunity (CRE, 1989a).

The survey of 116 of the 208 social services departments of England, Scotland and Wales (the majority serving the needs of significant minority ethnic group communities) found that only a third of departments had a written equal opportunities policy. Only 10 out of the 70 responding departments had introduced comprehensive ethnic monitoring, 18 had introduced some form of ethnic record-keeping, while in 8 cases such record-keeping applied only to specific control areas such as residential care.

Section 11 funding had been used primarily to appoint bilingual staff as interpreters and translators.[1] The survey revealed that over half of the departments had translated information about service provision into minority ethnic group languages, while 70 per cent used an interpreting service. A third of departments had appointed specialist 'race' advisers.

Some departments had adapted existing services to meet specific needs of minority ethnic groups: 39 had prioritized children in care; 23 had focused on campaigns for finding minority ethnic group foster/adoptive parents; and 17 had issued guidelines on the needs of children in care. However, only 25 per cent of the departments replied that they had written policies on minority ethnic group fostering and adoption. In establishing these priority areas, only 41 per cent of the responding departments indicated that they had consulted minority ethnic groups.

The CRE recommended that departments review their policies in consultation with minority ethnic groups, and introduce a systematic approach to the provision and delivery of services through an effective equal opportunities strategy. Such a strategy would include the recruitment of more minority ethnic group foster and adoptive families to ensure that same-'race' placements are possible in practice.

Alternative practices, such as transracial adoption and minority ethnic group placements, have provoked considerable criticism among minority communities:

> As the proportion of children in care who were black rose, itself indicating the tremendous socio-economic pressures upon the black family and the stigmatising attitudes of many white dominated welfare agencies, the black community came to believe that it was a net donor of its most precious assets to white families. The self-respect and sense of self-determination of the community has been threatened by a situation whereby most of its children in care were growing up either in white families or in white-controlled residential settings.

(Brent Social Services, 1985, pp. 6–7)

6.2 A paradox in client experience?

Evidence suggests that black and minority ethnic groups are under-represented as clients receiving the preventive and supportive elements of social services provision, but over-represented in those aspects of social services activity which involve social control functions and/or institutionalization (Roys, 1988, pp. 209–10). In Birmingham, for example, Duncan found that while Asian communities make up 30 per cent of the population, they comprise only 8 per cent of referrals to social services in an average month (Duncan, 1986, pp. 18–19).[2] A study of the minority ethnic group elderly in Handsworth found that relatively few black elderly people were coming to the notice of social services, while it was a myth to suppose that they were supported by a wide variety of community organizations and the extended family (West Midlands County Council, 1986, p. 48).

6.3 Referrals to care: the evidence

The CRE has persistently reported the disproportionately large number of minority ethnic group children taken into care during the 1980s (see, for example, CRE, 1990a, p. 67). In their 1983 evidence to the House of Commons Social Services Select Committee Inquiry into Children in Care, the CRE revealed the findings of a local study in a northern city which showed strikingly different rates between groups for children in care: 20.16 per 1,000 for white children, 24.32 per 1,000 for Afro-Caribbean children, but 142.24 per 1,000 for children of mixed parentage (CRE, 1983a, p. 4). In another local authority, Arnold found that 54 per cent of its children in care were black, although black children comprised only 47 per cent of the child population, and black people as a whole only 19 per cent of the population of the authority (Arnold, 1982, p. 99).

Barn's case study for *New Community* cited several research studies showing the disproportionate distributions of black children in care, findings which could not be fully explained by demographic factors (Barn, 1990, p. 230). Adams's (1981) study in Lambeth showed that 54 per cent of children in care were black and Wilkinson's (1982) study in Tower Hamlets showed that over 50 per cent of the children in their care were black. Barn's own research into the London Borough of 'Wenford' revealed that black children comprised 52 per cent of the borough's children in care though only 40 per cent of the population.[3] Over half of these children in care were Afro-Caribbean. This over-representation of black children in the care of Wenford's Social Services Department occurred in the five years preceding 1987. In contrast to other studies, Barn found that the differences applied when controlling for other factors such as age and gender of the children (Barn, 1990, pp. 237–40).

Barn examined the admission process of child care, comparing the 'care episode' of 294 black and 270 white children. The proportion of black children from single-parent families was 83 per cent, significantly higher than the 64 per cent of white children. Almost all the black children were born in Britain.

Of most interest here were conclusions about reasons for referral. More black children were referred because of family relationships and marital difficulties, financial reasons and material problems, and because of their mother's mental health (see *Table 6.1*); conversely, more white children were referred because of child (delinquent) behaviour and child (sexual) abuse.

Table 6.1: reasons for referrals being made to take children into care, by 'race', in percentages

Reason	Black	White	All
Family relationships	24	21	22
Financial/material circumstances	15	12	13
Parental neglect/inadequacy	21	33	27
Failure to thrive/medical health	1	6	3
Mother's mental health	11	5	8
Mother's ill-health	5	6	5
Homelessness/housing	11	11	11
Suspected child abuse	15	18	16
Child's behaviour	15	26	20
Total	(294)	(270)	(564)

The total refers to overall numbers in care. Actual percentages do not add up to 100 because of the multiplicity of reasons that could be recorded.
(Barn, 1990, p. 234)

Barn found significant differences when she examined the reasons why agencies referred black and white children. The differences are similar to those observed in Section 5.4 in relation to mental hospital referrals. For example, of the black delinquency referrals, 77 per cent came from the police compared with 35 per cent of the white delinquency referrals. In both groups the majority referred by the police were boys.

Barn discovered that children were admitted into care from situations where preventive strategies could have been attempted. Here again she found interesting differences between black and white children: lower proportions of white children were admitted for housing and financial reasons, and, where the reason for referral was mother's mental illness, greater proportions of black children were admitted into care than were actually initially referred. Barn found that black children entered care far more quickly than white children – on average nine months from referral for black children compared to over fifteen for white children. Black boys entered care at twice the rate of white boys. Comparing 'in care' age groups, Barn found that while black children of all age groups were over-represented in care, most of the 'in care' cohort were under the age of five when they entered into care. Barn's study also demonstrated the important role racial stereotypes play in pathologizing black families. It also showed the way in which black children's concerns have been omitted from the literature. Barn explained differences in the referral and admission patterns of black and white children in terms of social workers' perceptions of individual cases set against a context of the disadvantaged position of black families in the areas of housing and employment and the greater likelihood of such families needing social services help (Barn, 1990, pp. 229–45).

6.4 Social services staffing and training

> The recruitment of black social workers often makes only a marginal impact because their effectiveness is curtailed by being co-opted into existing power structures. In winning the battle for individual advancement they lose the war against racism.

(Jervis, 1986, p. 8)

In 1981 concern over the scarcity of qualified black social workers led to the ethnic monitoring of applicants for professional social work courses. In his 1988 review of social services provision for the Radical Statistics and Race Group (RSRG) Report, Roys revealed that preliminary monitoring showed a small rise in successful applicants from minority ethnic groups, from 7.9 per cent in 1981 to 11.8 per cent in 1984 (Bhat *et al.*, 1988, p. 226).

The Central Council for Education and Training in Social Work (CCETSW) has also addressed the curriculum of accredited social work courses. Their document *Teaching Social Work for a Multi-Racial Society* highlighted the inadequacy of much of this provision in relation to 'race' (CCETSW, 1983, pp. 15–20). In 1983, they concluded that the particular needs of the black population are frequently seen as marginal 'and so fail to reach many students, who may well complete their professional education with scarcely any teaching on multi-racial social work' (CCETSW, p. 22).

6.5 Barriers to benefits

6.5.1 Immigration policy

Caught up in a cycle of poverty (see Section 4), minority ethnic groups have been disadvantaged by immigration legislation in their eligibility for state benefits. Under the 1971 Immigration Act, increasing numbers of people have only been allowed entry into the UK on condition that they have 'no recourse to public funds' (Child Poverty Action Group, 1987, pp. 64–5). Under the 1988 Immigration Act, male Commonwealth citizens already settled in Britain when the 1971 Immigration Act came into force on 1 January 1973, must now prove they can maintain and accommodate their relatives arriving in the UK without having to resort to public funds (Gordon, 1989a, p. 4).

6.5.2 Discrimination in social security

Black and minority ethnic groups have also been disadvantaged by social security legislation. Under the 1980 Social Security Act, specific classes of immigrants were excluded by law from receiving benefits.[4] Under the 1986 Social Security Act, the introduction of a lower rate of benefit for single, childless people aged under 25 years on income support particularly affected those groups susceptible to relatively high rates of youth unemployment, and low parental income (see Sections 4 and 10.6). And the operation of the social fund and the greater emphasis on means-tested benefits potentially increases the risk of differential outcomes for minority ethnic groups through direct or indirect discriminatory practices by welfare staff, or decisions made on mistaken assumptions (CPAG, 1987, p. 67).

People from certain minority ethnic groups, whose first language is not English, often lose benefits because welfare offices cater badly for poor English speakers, according to a 1991 report published by the National Association of Citizens' Advice Bureaux (NACAB). The NACAB report revealed that such claimants can go for months without payment because forms are printed in English only (NACAB, 1991).

Section 4 traced the links between 'race' and poverty. It illustrated how people from minority ethnic groups were more likely to be both in low paid work and more frequently unemployed, especially younger age groups (see also Section 10.6). Such patterns affect their entitlement to all contributory benefits, such as retirement pensions. First-generation migrants may have entered pension schemes later in their working lives, and so do not have enough contributions to qualify for full pension rights (Oppenheim, 1990, pp. 88–91). Brown's (1984) study found that white people were six times more likely than black people to claim retirement or widow's pensions, while higher proportions of Asian and Caribbean people claimed unemployment benefits and family income supplements (see *Table 6.2*).

Table 6.2: support from state benefits by household type

Percentage of UK households in receipt of:	White	Caribbean	Asian
Child benefit	34	60	75
Unemployment benefit	7	17	16
Family income supplement	1	5	2
Supplementary benefit/Pension	14	20	11
Retirement/Widow's pension	35	6	6

(Brown, 1984, p. 242)

Notes

1   Section 11 funding refers to the section of the Local Government Act 1966 that empowers the Home Secretary to make payments to local authorities 'who in his opinion are required to make special provision in the exercise of any of their functions in consequence of the presence within the areas of substantial numbers of immigrants from the Commonwealth where language or custom differ from those of the community.' See Dorn and Hibbert (1987).

2   We need to be careful about conclusions we draw from this study. Duncan is not saying that Asian referrals *should* constitute 30 per cent of the population.

3   'Wenford' was a fictitious name used to refer to one of London's most economically deprived areas with one of the highest unemployment rates where people in work earned, on average, the lowest income in London. According to the 1981 census, 28 per cent of its residents were of New Commonwealth (NCWP) origin. Barn's 1987 case study encompassed all the components of 'care' – from voluntary care, interim care orders, through to full care orders and wardships (Barn, 1990, pp. 238–9).

4   For a fuller discussion see CPAG (1987) pp. 64–7.

7 'RACE' AND HOUSING

One of the greatest obstacles to progress in the elimination of racial discrimination is getting white-run housing institutions to acknowledge that racism and racial disadvantage exist. Despite all the evidence, many housing managers, officers and councillors will categorically deny that racial discrimination could exist within their own organisation.

(Phillips, 1989, p. 141)

7.1 The context: policy, 'race' and housing status

There were significant shifts in state housing policy and tenurial provision in the 1980s (for example, the sale of council houses). There was also a dramatic reduction in government spending on housing. In February 1991, Norman Lamont, the Chancellor of the Exchequer, told Nicholas Ridley (Conservative MP, Cirencester and Tewkesbury) that government spending on housing had fallen by more than one half in real terms since 1979 (*Independent,* 13 February 1991).

In the 1990s Britain's minority ethnic groups live in better housing conditions than they did in the 1950s. Nevertheless, major disparities in housing outcomes still remain, and housing quality remains a problem for many. During the late 1980s and early 1990s, a series of Commission for Racial Equality (CRE) formal reports and investigations across a range of tenures further pointed to the overt and covert processes, practices and procedures, including institutional racism, which help create and sustain differences in minority ethnic group housing outcomes.[1]

This section will focus on some of the more recent evidence for differential housing outcomes for minority ethnic groups within each tenure, explore evidence linking 'race' with homelessness, and report further evidence on racial harassment, particularly as it relates to council tenant eviction (see also Section 3.4).

In 1987, reviewing research into minority ethnic group housing outcomes, Phillips concluded that while the statistics showed an absolute improvement in minority ethnic group housing standards, they also revealed 'a pattern of entrenched housing inequality' (1987, p. 108). For those minority ethnic group households who had acquired decent accommodation, Phillips noted that: 'the fight has been hard won. Success in terms of housing outcome cannot always be equated with equality of treatment. The price of good housing has often been high in both financial and emotional terms' (ibid., p. 108). Phillips summarized the differential nature of minority ethnic group housing outcomes by 1987 as follows:

> West Indians and Asians are more likely to live in pre-1945 dwellings (60 per cent and 74 per cent respectively) than the white population (50 per cent). They are also twice as likely to live in the terraced property so commonly associated with inner city residence. Overcrowding remains a particular problem amongst Asians (35 per cent live in overcrowded conditions compared to 3 per cent of whites) and, in recent years, homelessness has increased greatly ... Black people may now have a bath and W.C., but they are also likely to be the casualties of other inequalities in housing provision.

> In the 1980s then, the NCWP minorities still live in significantly worse quality housing and in poorer, less popular areas than the white British population. This holds both across and within tenures. Indeed, the high level of owner occupation amongst Asians (72 per cent as against 59 per cent of the general population) provides no guarantee of good housing ... the prevailing trend in many cities over the last two decades has been one of growing residential segregation between NCWP minorities and whites, with the former becoming increasingly over-represented in the poorest areas. This is particularly true of the Asian population, whose potential for residential mixing has been reduced by their relative absence from council housing. As analyses of local authority data have shown, however, segregation within the public sector itself is all too prevalent and inequality prevails ... Within this sector, movement away from the inner city cannot necessarily be equated with access to decent housing.

(Phillips, 1987, p. 108)

Table 7.1 focuses on intra-ethnic differences in tenure, comparing the years 1981 and 1988. In 1988, West Indian households were nearly four times as likely to rent accommodation from a local authority than households where there was an Indian head, and nearly twice as likely as those from white ethnic groups. Between 1981 and 1988 the proportion of all minority ethnic groups buying a property with a mortgage increased, but increased most for Pakistani/Bangladeshi minorities.

Table 7.1: tenure by ethnic group of head of household in England, 1981 and 1988, in percentages

| | Owner ocupied | | | | Rented | | | |
| | owned occupied | | with mortgage | | local authority | | private | |
	1981	1988	1981	1988	1981	1988	1981	1988
White	25	26	32	40	29	23	13	11
Other ethnic groups of which:	18	15	35	44	28	25	18	16
Indian	26	25	49	55	13	11	11	9
Pakistani/ Bangladeshi	32	20	39	54	18	15	11	11
West Indian	8	7	28	35	47	43	17	15
Other or mixed	15	9	26	39	28	26	31	25
Not stated	22	29	27	33	32	18	19	21
All ethnic groups	25	26	32	40	29	23	13	12

(Adapted from Central Statistical Office, 1991, p. 146)

7.2 Local authority housing

Between 1976 and 1989 house building completions by local authorities (and new towns) fell from 124,512 to 13,555, with the numbers of dwellings with three or more bedrooms falling from 42 per cent of the housebuilding completions in 1976 to only 22 per cent in 1989 (Central Statistical Office, 1991, p. 137, paras 8.4 and 8.5). The changing distribution of dwelling size is linked to the changing structure of households, but, as Section 1 reveals, recent provision does not closely correspond to the needs of minority ethnic group households, such as large families. Moreover, during the 1980s almost one and a half million local authority and new town dwellings were sold to occupiers, much of it stock of good quality in locations popular with white applicants for rented accommodation.[2]

Evidence of local authority housing disadvantage for minority ethnic groups is reviewed by Ginsburg (1992).[3] In 1989 formal investigations by the CRE, conducted in a variety of towns and cities in the UK, showed that disadvantages often accrued despite the existence of equal opportunities policies. For example, an Edinburgh study found that unlawful discrimination did occur and that a disproportionate number of black tenants were allocated in the unpopular area of Wester Hailes, where 82 per cent of black tenants, as opposed to 50 per cent elsewhere, had experienced racial harassment (MacEwan and Verity, 1989). In the London Borough of Southwark, the CRE found the borough indirectly discriminated against minority ethnic group tenants when it gave new properties from a major improvement programme mainly to white tenants (CRE, 1990d).

A 1988 CRE report into the London Borough of Tower Hamlets showed how Bangladeshis were more likely to be allocated the worst housing; how Bangladeshis ended up in the borough's poorest temporary bed and break-fast accommodation; how Bangladeshis waited longer than whites to be allocated housing; how emergency housing for those made homeless by fire or vandalism was made available more quickly for whites; and how the council discriminated against Bangladeshi families when they applied for housing. The report found that of three estates examined in the borough, the two with the lowest housing standards housed five times the number of Asian tenants as would be expected given their proportion in the borough's population (CRE, 1988c).

7.3 Owner occupation

Differential outcomes to minority ethnic groups in the owner-occupied sector has been the subject of much detailed research (Ginsburg, 1992; CRE, 1985b; Smith, 1989). Evidence in the late 1980s particularly focused on discriminatory practices of estate agencies in the housing market (Sarre *et al.*, 1989, ch. 7). Two CRE investigations, one into an estate agency in Clapham and Wandsworth, the other into an Oldham agency, resulted in the issuing of non-discrimination notices, and further highlighted the ways in which estate agencies contravene the 1976 Race Relations Act (CRE, 1988c; 1990e). The Oldham investigation revealed how one agency:

- discriminated against vendors of properties in areas of Asian population;
- segregated purchasers on racial grounds;
- accepted discriminatory instructions from vendors;
- discriminated against Asian clients in the provision of mortgage facilities.

On the positive side, the estate agency business has begun to 'put its own house in order' by developing equal opportunities policies. For example, another CRE report documents the responses of two estate agencies follow-ing advice that their branches might possibly be engaged in practices contravening the Race Relations Act 1976 (CRE, 1990c). One is among the ten largest firms of estate agents in the UK with 800 branches and 6,000 employees in 1990; the other is a smaller company operating in the Greater Manchester area. Both set up equal opportunities policies and implemented them within a short space of time. Their progress is being monitored. Following the publication of the CRE code of practice in the owner-occupied housing sector, such initiatives to combat institutional racism may be expected to occur elsewhere among housing gatekeepers (CRE, 1991b).

7.4 Housing associations

Partly in response to cuts in council housing, minority ethnic groups have increasingly looked to improve their housing situation in the voluntary sector. The Federation of Black Housing Organisations (FBHO) have broadened housing access for minority ethnic groups during the 1980s by developing links with housing associations and monitoring outcomes in the voluntary sector (Phillips, R., 1986). However, despite the establishment of equal opportunity policies as an integral part of housing association activity, as well as Housing Corporation grants to newly registered black groups, and the allocation of £100,000 a year to encourage black participation in housing associations, progress to reduce discriminatory effects remains slow. Of 2,600 housing organizations registered with the Housing Corporation in 1986, only twelve were controlled by black people, and only six owned their own property. Studies in Bradford and Rochdale have shown the potential role housing associations could play in bridging the gap in low income housing provision for minority ethnic group families (Brimacombe, 1991). Existing research suggests, however, that housing associations inherit many of the features of local authorities in the way in which they treat minority ethnic group applicants and tenants. Research undertaken into four Scottish housing associations in the late 1980s, and published in 1989, showed that black people were disproportionately found in below-standard housing in areas where locally-based housing associations had been operating for twenty years (Dalton and Daghlian, 1989).

A CRE investigation in Liverpool found that under housing allocations made by the city council white people were twice as likely as black people to get a house, four times more likely to get a new house, twice as likely to get a centrally heated home, and four times more likely to get their own garden (CRE, 1989b). The investigation followed a CRE study of Liverpool City Council in 1984. This found that black households received lower quality council housing than white households. The council had established an equal opportunities policy in 1981, employed a community relations officer in the housing department since 1982, and developed what the CRE called a 'radical' policy on racial harassment since 1983. The 1984 report had recommended that the council introduce minority ethnic group monitoring and training, improve information provision, broaden systematic in-service training, employ specialist staff and increase the proportion of black staff in the housing department (CRE, 1984b).

In looking at housing association nominations, the 1989 Liverpool report found evidence which mirrored that discovered for Liverpool's council housing in 1984. Two thousand housing association case histories were studied during 1987 and 1988. Black housing association nominees consistently received poorer properties than white nominees across all quality measures. The CRE could not explain the differential outcomes in terms of area preferences, economic circumstances, or household size. A non-discrimination notice was issued against Liverpool City Council. Another study, by the FBHO in the mid-1980s, found that, of 1,289 sheltered accommodation places for the elderly provided by Liverpool City Council and housing associations, only two were occupied by Asian or Afro-Caribbean households (FBHO, 1986).

7.5 Private rented housing

Racism in the private rented sector has a long history.[4] While signs stating 'no blacks, no Irish, no dogs' may have disappeared since the introduction of 'race' relations legislation, evidence at the beginning of the 1990s continues to show that racial bias persists in the rented sector, albeit at more subtle levels. The CRE report *Sorry, It's Gone* showed that one in five accommodation agencies in thirteen different locations discriminated against minority ethnic group applicants (CRE, 1990f). In Ealing almost half of the agencies were found to discriminate, and in Bristol a third. The report showed how agents would deny minority ethnic group applicants access to private rented property, while readily referring white people of identical status and means. The report also showed that one in twenty private landlords and landladies discriminated. The 'good news', CRE concluded, was the relative absence of discriminatory practices by owners of guest houses and small hotels. However, while the old days of blatant racial discrimination had largely disappeared, the CRE maintained that the level of racial discrimination nevertheless remained 'worryingly high':

> what we found was not discrimination at second hand, where agencies were following discriminatory instructions from landlords and landladies, but rather discriminatory decisions taken by agency staff themselves, directly, through a mixture of ignorance, racial stereotyping or plain racial bigotry.

(CRE, 1990f, p. 5)

In a press release launching the report, the chair of the CRE, Michael Day, described the findings of the investigation as 'shameful, but not surprising'. He called for government legislation to ensure that all accommodation agencies are licensed with a code of conduct and their performance is monitored.[5] Commenting on the report, the London Housing Unit said that racism in the private rented housing sector helped to ensure that three times more black people than white were likely to become homeless.[6] There remains, also, the problem of the poor quality of much private rented accommodation. For example, a study into Kensington and Chelsea, the London borough with the highest private rented sector, found that its 214,000 minority ethnic groups – mainly Filipino, Moroccan, and Latin American migrant workers – lived in the worst private rented housing in the country.[7]

7.6 'Race' and homelessness

Ethnic minorities are represented among the homeless at a disproportionately high level, and suffer racial discrimination as well as all the other problems associated with homelessness.

(CRE, 1988c, p. 7)

The rise in homelessness throughout the 1980s reflects changes in housing policy. Greve and Currie (1990) estimated that, in 1989, 356,000 households, or 686,000 people, could be defined as homeless.[8] The risk of becoming homeless is considerably higher for people on low income, single parents, and members of minority ethnic groups (Oppenheim, 1990, p. 53). In 1988 research in London showed that minority ethnic group households are up to four times as likely to become homeless as white households (National Association of Citizen's Advice Bureaux (NACAB), 1988; Sexty, 1990, pp. 45–6) The CRE investigation (1988c) found that the majority of the 1300 homeless in Tower Hamlets were Bangladeshi. The number of Bangladeshis on the homeless lists was also swollen by the borough's policy on divided families and immigration. A father who wanted to bring his wife and children to join him in England from Bangladesh could not be actively considered for housing until they arrived, making them automatically homeless on arrival (CRE, 1988c).

The young, especially those who are single, are particularly vulnerable to homelessness. A survey of 24 London boroughs in 1989 revealed the extent of an escalating problem. In Brent and Southwark a disproportionate number of the single homeless were young black people. In Newham, black homeless single people made up 56 per cent of referrals to hostels, 40 per cent of the referrals being under 18. The survey revealed that an increasing proportion of the single homeless were women, especially young Asians (Single Homeless in London and London Housing Unit, 1989).[9]

The negative impact of homelessness on education and life chances has been well documented. For example, a survey by HMIs found that homeless children tended not to be enrolled at school, were frequently absent, performed relatively poorly in class, and suffered from low self-esteem and expectations.[10]

7.7 *Racial harassment and 'racist' tenants*

Sections 3.4 and 3.5 looked at racial harassment in the home and at school. One of the problems confronting housing departments such as Tower Hamlets, where the Bangladeshi population alone rose from 12,000 to 40,000 between 1982 and 1987, is what kind of policy to adopt to ameliorate homelessness, or reduce the concentration of Bangladeshis in particular areas. Here the issue of 'racist' council tenants has to be confronted. The CRE report on the borough highlighted the level of racial harassment and abuse and the frequency of racist attacks on Bangladeshis living in the worst accommodation and on those rehoused in 'white areas'.[11]

Recording the prolonged torment of an East London Asian family who were the victims of racial harassment, John Pilger examined the testimony of a teenage girl through her diary entries on racial attacks on her family home. The girl, Nasreen, wrote to Mrs Thatcher during 1983:

Dear Margaret Thatcher,

I am sorry to say you don't understand our matter ... you don't care if we get beaten up, do you? My mother has asthma and she had to stay to 11am watching through the window because me and my brother and sister has to go to school. I can't stay home to look after my mother because I got exams to worry about. We have no money to repair our house since the kids in the street have damaged it.

We are asking for your help, not your money, Mrs Thatcher.

Yours sincerely,

Nasreen

(John Pilger, 'Nasreen, voice of outrage from a house under seige', *Independent,* 2 February 1987)

A reply came not from the then Prime Minister, but from Mr C. D. Inge at the Home Office. Mr Inge urged the family to keep reporting every incident to the police 'even if the police are unable to take any action'. He then apologized for not being 'able to give you a more helpful reply' (*Independent,* 2 February 1987).

Until the mid-1980s the response of most councils to allegations of racial harassment or attack on white estates has been to treat them as private disputes between neighbours. In the worse cases, black tenants are transferred back to other areas for their own safety – often back to overcrowded estates with high concentrations of minority ethnic group tenants. In 1984 Newham became the first local authority to evict a white family for persistent and violent harassment of their Asian neighbours.[12] By the end of 1987, six cases had been brought against white tenants, all in London, but only three had been successful. Councils began to include the perpetration of racial harassment as a specific ground for eviction in tenancy agreements. By 1988 over half of the London boroughs had introduced such clauses in their agreements. However, problems with legal interpretation and definitions of racial harassment have resulted in few councils taking action, further raising the levels of disillusionment in minority ethnic group communities.

Figure 7.1: Tower Hamlets' tenants demand to be transferred to safer housing

Notes

1   The research evidence on 'institutional racism and racism in housing' is substantial, and there is a developing literature on policy implementation in the area of equal opportunities. For a fuller discussion of institutional racism in housing and a review of some of the evidence that emerged in the 1970s and 1980s see Ginsburg (1992) (Open University course ED356 Reader 3). For a useful discussion of the particular housing needs and experiences of minority ethnic group women – usually ignored in research – see Sexty (1990) ch. 3. For more details of evidence for racism in housing see CRE (1988a; 1989b; 1990b); MacEwan and Verity (1989); Dalton and Daghlian (1989). For information on equal opportunities policies in relation to housing see Phillips (1989) p. 142; CRE (1989c; 1990c; 1991b).

2   See Forrest and Murie (1990, p. 212) and 'Lending to council house tenants', Nationwide Anglia Building Society, May 1990. No breakdowns were available on house sales and ethnic background at the time of publication.

3   See also Henderson and Karn (1984); CRE (1984b); Phillips, D. (1986); Sarre *et al.* (1989) ch. 5.

4   For a useful review of landlord discrimination see Smith and Hill (1991).

5   CRE Press Release, 13 September 1990.

6   *Independent*, 14 September 1990.

7   Grant (1989). The 1987 London Earnings Survey showed that the borough had the lowest pay in London but that council rents were the highest.

8   Official statistics relate to a flow of households rehoused during a year, not to the number of households without a home at any one time.

9   See also *Roof*, January/February 1989, p. 10; Sexty (1990) p. 47.

10 *Independent*, 6 August 1990.

11 *Independent*, 2 September 1988.

12 See Phillips, R. (1986) p. 13. For a fascinating discussion of council tenants' experiences of and attitudes to racism see *Tenants Tackle Racism*, Dame Colet House/Limehouse Fields Tenants Association and Tower Hamlets Tenants Federation (1986).

8 'RACE' AND THE CRIMINAL JUSTICE SYSTEM

8.1 Inequalities in judicial provision

8.1.1 The judiciary

At a meeting with barristers and solicitors in London on 6 November 1990 the Lord Chancellor, Lord Mackay of Clashern, was reported as saying:

> The bench in 10 or 20 years time should look very different in terms of racial and sexual composition from that of today ... Nothing would be worse for the reputation of the judiciary in this country than for me to lower standards for appointment to the judiciary simply to ensure a different racial or sexual mix ... It is worth stressing that it is not a function of the judiciary to be representative of the population as a whole.

(*Independent*, 7 November 1990)

A month later in the House of Commons, Sir Patrick Mayhew, the Attorney General, replying to a question from Mr Brian Sedgemore MP about the ethnic composition of the judiciary, said:

> Candidates for judicial appointment are considered on their merits regardless of sex or ethnic origin. The Lord Chancellor has, however, repeatedly made clear his wish to appoint more women and members of ethnic minorities to judicial office ... At the moment, there are relatively few women and ethnic minority candidates in the legal profession in the appropriate age groups with the right experience ... It is impossible, however, to predict the composition of the pool of suitably qualified candidates for judicial office, or the number of appointments needed, 10 years ahead, and it would therefore be inappropriate to set targets.

(*Hansard*, 1990, p. 113)

Figures produced by the Law Society in March 1991 revealed a huge disparity in the proportions of men, women and members of minority ethnic groups on the bench, and the pool of potential candidates from which that bench is selected (see *Table 8.1*).

Table 8.1: the make-up of the judiciary in England and Wales

Judges	Total	Women	%	Minority ethnic groups	%
House of Lords	10	0	0%	0	0%
Court of Appeal	27	2	7.41%	0	0%
High Court	83	2	1.66%	0	0%
Circuit judges	429	19	4.4%	1	0.2%
Recorders (part-time)	744	42	5.7%	3	0.4%
Assistant recorders (part-time)	443	27	6.0%	2	0.4%
The candidates					
Practising barristers	5,994	1,246	21.0%	376	6.0%
Practising solicitors	54,734	12,683	23.2%	709*	1.3%

* 16,622 respondents to the Law Society survey declined to specify their ethnic group
(Based on Lord Chancellor's Department 1991; Law Society 1989–90; Bar Council 1989–90)

Of a total of 1,736 full- and part-time judicial posts, 92 were held by women and only 6 by people from minority ethnic groups. The Law Society is concerned that the current appointment system may be illegal under the 1976 Race Relations Act because of its dependence on 'word of mouth' selection which may indirectly discriminate against minority group candidates (*Independent*, 27 February and 8 March 1991).

8.1.2 Jury composition

In the early 1990s, the Lord Chancellor's Department examined the make-up of juries to assess the justification for fears that minority ethnic group defendants are being placed at a disadvantage in criminal trials because the juries do not reflect the ethnic composition of British society. The essence of the jury system is random selection, but in recent years this system has consistently failed to achieve jury panels that reflect ethnic composition. Black solicitors claim that the abolition in January 1989 of the defence's right to challenge jurors pre-emptorily has exacerbated the problem.

In a major study, Baldwin and McConville (1979) examined the jury composition in 720 trials in Birmingham and London. They identified 'immense' under-representation on juries of people from black Commonwealth countries. Only 28 out of 3,912 jurors selected for 326 Birmingham juries (0.7 per cent) were of West Indian or Asian origin.[1] In the 1990s the problem remains. In July 1990 the CRE's Chief Executive commented:

People from ethnic minority communities appear to be under–represented among jurors ... and heavily over–represented among defendants. This imbalance is bound to undermine the confidence of these communities in the criminal justice system as a whole. There are difficulties in achieving ethnically mixed juries, but they are not insuperable ... We believe the restoration of preemptory challenge would probably assist the objective ... [but it] would need to be underpinned ... by a right for all defendants to a racially mixed jury, together with a clear declaration that all criminal justice agencies had a statutory duty to operate on a non-discriminatory basis.

(Peter Saunders, 'Ethnic balance among juries', *Independent,* 2 July 1990)

8.1.3 The magistracy

Magistrates are responsible for 98 per cent of criminal charges dealt with by the courts of England and Wales. The lay magistracy is supposed to reflect the community which it serves, but there are still relatively few black magistrates (see *Table 8.2*).

Table 8.2: black people employed in the criminal justice system

Probation service	1.9%
Police	0.9%
Solicitors	1.3%
Magistrates	1.9%
Prison staff	0.6%

Note: uses National Association of Probation Officer data
(McDermott, 1990, p. 215)

In 1970 there were only 15 black magistrates in England and Wales. By 1979 this figure had risen to 115: by 1986 it had trebled to 325 of whom 86 were women.[2] By 1 January 1988 the number stood at 455 – 1.9 per cent of the 23,730 active magistrates in England and Wales. Despite the rise since 1970, minority ethnic groups are still under-represented among the magistracy. This is the case especially for black women – female magistrates accounted for only 1.15 per cent of the total. During the 1980s, however, the proportion of black magistrates appointed rose gradually. In 1980, 1.8 per cent of magistracy appointments were to black people: by 1986 the proportion had risen to 4.6 per cent. In the late 1980s, the proportion of black appointments to the magistracy in the age range 35–54 was *higher* than their distribution in the population as a whole.[3] In April 1991 Richard Grobler, an official in the Lord Chancellor's Department, claimed that 6 per cent of appointments to the magistracy were to black people (more than their representation in the population of England and Wales). Grobler told the *Independent*, 'We do try and target particular groups – for instance by advertising in the *Caribbean Times* – to improve the balance of the benches.'[4]

8.1.4 Solicitors and barristers

There were relatively few minority ethnic group solicitors in 1988 – only 618 out of 48,494, or 1.28 per cent (see *Table 8.2*). They are located disproportionately in small practices: 22 per cent operate on their own compared with 9 per cent of all solicitors, and more than 80 per cent work in firms with fewer than four solicitors compared with 56 per cent in total.[5]

According to research conducted at Brunel University, significant barriers to entry into the legal profession operate against minority ethnic group law students seeking to become solicitors.[6] It found that, on average, minority ethnic group candidates made almost twice as many applications to solicitors' firms for articles as their white counterparts and they received proportionately fewer interview offers. After interview, 12 per cent of minority ethnic group students received more offers than rejections compared to 44 per cent of white students. The former were also found to have a poor chance of finding a job with a commercial law firm, where the salaries are higher than in other areas of legal practice.

Firms were found to operate a policy based not on 'race', but on what they saw as 'excellence'. They may, for example, require applicants to have an Oxbridge degree or a 'prestigious' educational background. Minority ethnic group candidates were found to be disproportionately disadvantaged by such criteria. The study concluded that solicitors' firms needed to reappraise their selection criteria and procedures radically. It also recommended that universities and polytechnics place less emphasis on A-level grades as the entry qualification for law degree courses and extend part-time and day-release study for such courses. In 1991, another study examining the implications of the Law Society-controlled College of Law clearing house system for allocating places on solicitors' finals courses found that the two entry criteria used – whether students have been offered articles (professional training) by law firms and the class of degree they are likely to obtain – may potentially prevent black law graduates studying at polytechnics from entering finals courses.

Minority ethnic group barristers fare better than solicitors: but they make up no more than 5 per cent of the profession. However, more than 75 per cent of minority ethnic group barristers work in only 19 sets of chambers. In 1990 the majority of chambers contained no black barristers. In May 1991 the Bar Council, the profession's governing body, approved guidelines which instructed chambers of barristers that at least 5 per cent of their members and pupils should come from minority ethnic groups. It also asked clerks, the

Crown Prosecution Service, government departments, local authorities and large companies to ensure that at least 5 per cent of the work sent to chambers be directed to black and Asian barristers. The Bar Council also announced their intention to monitor the programme, appoint an equal opportunities officer, and produce a directory of black barristers.[7] The first black woman Queens Counsel was appointed on 28 March 1991.[8] In October 1991 the Bar Council adopted a race relations policy to encourage more people from minority ethnic groups into the profession.[9]

8.1.5 Probation officers

Black people are also under-represented in the probation service. In 1985, 127 out of 6,800 probation officers – less than 2 per cent – were black. The British Council of Churches (BCC) report which disclosed these figures remarked with regret that this was one area that showed little increase in black representation, 'partly due to black officers leaving in disgust or despair' (British Council of Churches, 1990, p. 3). A 1988 National Association of Probation Officers (NAPO) report revealed that only 1.9 per cent of probation officers were from minority ethnic groups (see *Table 8.2*).

8.2 Differential outcomes: arrests, remands, prisoners and prisons

In August 1989 Stephen Shaw, director of the Prison Reform Trust (PRT), claimed that if white people were jailed at the same rate as black people the total prison population of the UK would be 300,000. It is under 50,000. The PRT calculated that the black imprisonment rate for England and Wales was then 775 per 100,000 of the population compared to 98.2 per 100,000 for the population as a whole. The PRT figures indicate that black people could be eight times more likely than white people to end up in prison. Shaw concluded:

> Black people are more likely than their white counterparts to be stopped by the police. If stopped, they are more likely to be arrested. If arrested, more likely to be charged. If charged, more likely to be remanded in custody, and if convicted, more likely to receive a sentence of imprisonment.

> (Quoted in T. Kirby, 'Black jail figures would shame South Africa', *Independent*, 7 August 1989)

An investigation by the National Association for the Care and Resettlement of Offenders (NACRO) in 1990 showed black people to be more vulnerable at most stages of the criminal justice system than white people. They were more likely to be stopped and searched by police, to be prosecuted and to receive a prison sentence than their white counterparts. They were also more likely to be charged immediately and less likely to be cautioned.[10] A Home Office spokesperson commented, 'while it may be hard to prove discrimination in any one particular case, the figures would tend to show there is some kind of subtle discrimination' (Independent, 14 January 1991).

In 1986 it was estimated that 63 per cent of black youths had experienced some adversarial contact with the police, compared with 35 per cent of white people of the same age. The Forum for the Advancement of Training and Education for the Black Unemployed (FATEBU) reported that, given the trends of the late 1980s, one in ten black males are likely to be imprisoned by their twenty-first birthday (Burns, 1990, p. 7).

According to a NAPO report, black people made up 20 per cent of the remand population of England and Wales and 38 per cent of the remand population in London in 1987–8 (compared to 4.4 per cent of the general population). Afro-Caribbean defendants on remand were twice as likely to be acquitted as their white counterparts. The assistant general secretary of NAPO commented, 'The evidence strongly suggests that the system is discriminatory.' NAPO also revealed that in 23 prisons more than one-quarter of the inmates were black. Their data (see Table 8.2) showed that at that time the professional groups involved in the remand process had poor records of recruiting black staff (Fletcher, 1988, pp. 8–11).

In 1991 black people comprised 15 per cent of the prison population of England and Wales: 66 per cent of black people under sentence were of West Indian, Guyanese or African origin. While offence categories varied between the groups, certain offences stood out in the 1991 figures. For example, whereas only 5.6 per cent of whites were under sentence for drug offences, the figure for West Indians/Guyanese/Africans was 22.5 per cent, and for Indians/Pakistanis/Bangladeshis 31.3 per cent.[11]

Black women are more likely to be in prison than black men: 24 per cent of women imprisoned or remanded in custody before trial in 1989 were from minority ethnic groups (NACRO, 1991).[12] A NACRO study in 1987 revealed that women were more than twice as likely to be sent to prison as they were in 1977. On 30 June 1987, 26 per cent of women in custody whose records were known had no previous convictions, compared with 8 per cent of men. Overall, sentenced black prisoners had fewer previous convictions than white prisoners punished for the same type of offence. This study also showed that black people were significantly less likely to have been granted bail (NACRO, 1988).[13] Commenting on the report, NACRO's director said:

> These figures do not show that black people are more prone to crime than white people, but they do suggest that black people who offend are more likely to go to prison ... Some useful first steps have been taken by

the prison service, the police, the probation service, and the legal profession: but a comprehensive strategy is essential if we are to ensure that the administration of justice is fair, and seen to be fair in our multi-racial society.

(Vivien Stern, Director of NACRO, quoted in the *Independent*, 14 June 1988)

In a three-year study of five Midland prisons, McDermott (1990) argued that perceived racism is an instrinsic part of the prison service.[14] When all prisoners in her survey were asked to evaluate whether or not they thought staff were racist in their attitudes, nearly three out of five blacks, almost half the Asians and a third of whites thought the prison staff were racist. But the racism applies also to 'the cons'. One of McDermott's prisoners explained the subtleties behind some staff and prisoner interactions:

There's a lot of racism here, open and unopen. You can break it up into the screws and the cons. The cons are racist between themselves. They'll say nigger this and nigger that, but it doesn't really go further because a lot of the black guys are physically a lot bigger. Now the screws do it openly, but they do it in such a way that it's unopen; like it's supposed to be a joke. But what can you say or do about it? You can't complain to the Governor because his officers can't lie ... You can't cross them because you know you'll come out the worst. They have the power.

(McDermott, 1990, p. 221)

In July 1991 the Institute of Race Relations (IRR) recommended that the government establish a Royal Commission to investigate deaths in custody. The call for a Standing Commission on Deaths in Custody followed extensive research into 75 black people who have died in police, prison and hospital care between 1970 and 1990. Only one of the 75 cases resulted in a prosecution of the police and in only one case did the family of the deceased receive compensation. The 75 deaths included many people who were diagnosed as mentally ill: others were refugees claiming asylum. The IRR report concluded that consideration of the unequal treatment of black people at all stages of the criminal justice system should form the basis of a Royal Commission (IRR, 1991).

In spite of efforts to recruit minority ethnic group members on to important public boards and committees associated with the prison system, representation on these bodies has not caught up with black representation in the prison population. For example, in 1987 NACRO reported that of the 67 Parole Board members only 7.5 per cent were from minority ethnic groups; of the Local Review Committee, only 5.7 per cent; and of the members of the Board of Visitors, only 9 per cent (McDermott, 1990, p. 216).

8.3 Education, training and black offenders

According to FATEBU, the overwhelming majority of people known to the prison and probation services are unemployed and have had very poor previous experiences of education. In the early 1990s FATEBU, NACRO and the Prison Service's Education Branch launched a series of individually tailored schemes to allow the courts to consider community based sentences, instead of custody, especially for young black offenders (Burns, 1990, p. 8). Examining such initiatives, Burns observed:

> One of the central issues remaining is that in all parts of the criminal justice system black offenders are overwhelmingly dealt with by white staff. The system clearly needs to become more responsive to black organisations and attempt to involve black people much more in its institutions. This process should inform our education and training activities. Black educators as well as consumers have a part to play in that change.

(Burns, 1990, p. 8)

8.4 Police and policing

8.4.1 The thin blue line: black police officer recruitment

BBC1's *Nine O'Clock News*, 8 April 1991, ten years after the Brixton disturbances, reported that only 12 out of 300 officers in the Brixton force were black. A survey conducted by *Today* newspaper in the autumn of 1990 revealed that of our 51 police forces, only 1,308 police officers, 0.9 per cent, were drawn from minority ethnic groups (see *Table 8.3*).

According to this survey, the proportions for the large urban connurbations were: West Midlands 2.41 per cent; Metropolitan Police, including the City of London, 1.63 per cent; West Yorkshire 1.56 per cent (where the pool of black potential recruits in the appropriate age cohorts is over 15 per cent); Greater Manchester 1.54 per cent; and Merseyside 0.9 per cent. Bedfordshire with 2.96 per cent and Leicestershire with 2.53 per cent were the most successful forces in terms of black recruitment. Dyfed-Powys, Lincolnshire, and Norfolk, all areas with small minority ethnic group communities, had no black officers.

Table 8.3: numbers of black and Asian police officers in Britain

Force	Total strength	Minority ethnic group officers	Force	Total strength	Minority ethnic group officers
Metropolitan Police (including City of London)	24,468	463	Lancashire	3,167	18
			Leicestershire	1,743	44
Avon and Somerset	3,080	20	Lincolnshire	1,197	0
Bedfordshire	1,047	31	Lothian and Borders	2,440	2
Cambridgeshire	1,187	20	Merseyside	4,810	43
Central Scotland	638	1	Norfolk	1,400	0
Dumfries and Galloway	363	0	Northampton	1,141	18
Dyfed, Powys	943	0	Northern Scotland	624	0
Cheshire	1,865	4	North Wales	1,327	1
Cleveland	1,497	9	Nottinghamshire	2,344	50
Cumbria	1,144	2	North Yorkshire	1,379	2
Derbyshire	1,793	23	Northumbria	3,593	12
Dorset	1,281	3	Royal Ulster Constabulary	8,260	6
Devon and Cornwall	2,846	2	South Yorkshire	2,937	21
Durham	1,375	3	Staffordshire	2,202	17
Essex	2,902	18	Strathclyde	6,825	14
Gloucestershire	1,164	11	Suffolk	1,204	6
Greater Manchester	7,008	108	Sussex	2,960	9
			Surrey	1,659	9
Grampian	1,158	1	Tayside	1,036	3
Gwent	1,002	4	Thames Valley	3,685	47
Hertfordshire	1,658	19	Warwickshire	1,007	9
Humberside	1,989	3	West Mercia	2,023	19
Hampshire	3,173	9	West Midlands	6,859	165
Kent	2,991	20	West Yorkshire	5,279	82
			Wiltshire	1,098	9

(Today, 2 October 1990)

Since the mid-1980s, police forces have become more engaged in recruitment drives directed at black and minority ethnic group communities, using targeting in specific localities, often linked to local minority ethnic group organizations and backed by advertisements in minority ethnic group media (Oakley, 1989). In 1989 only 27 black or Asian men and 8 women joined the Metropolitan Police.[15] In January 1990, they announced measures to increase black recruitment. The minimum height ruling for police officers (5ft 8in for men and 5ft 4in for women), which was felt to exclude recruitment of many people from Asia and the Indian subcontinent, was scrapped.[16] The Metropolitan Police also announced a television advertising campaign – for the first time in fifteen years.

8.4.2 Police career prospects

A CRE study in 1988 revealed that black officers are very poorly represented in ranks above that of police constable, and scarcely at all above sergeant. Black representation among non-uniformed police staff was also disproportionately low (Oakley, 1989). A report for the Commons Home Affairs Committee in autumn 1989 noted that there were no black or Asian officers in the ranks of chief superintendent or above.[17] At the end of 1989, the highest ranking black police officer was a Leicestershire superintendent. There is also evidence that wastage for black recruits is higher than for whites.[18] In 1989, 26 out of 35 black or Asian recruits to the Metropolitan Police left the force.[19]

8.4.3 Racism within the force

It's [racism] routine in some parts of the service. If it's routine in the force, it's almost certainly routine to some degree with some police forces to members of the public.

(John Newing, Chief Constable of Derbyshire, quoted in the *Independent,* 1 December 1990)

Two landmark industrial tribunal cases in 1990–1 highlighted the extent to which racist abuse and banter is rooted in police force culture. A Nottingham industrial tribunal found that PC Surinder Singh was unlawfully discriminated against by Nottinghamshire Constabulary in his training for the CID, and in the force's decision not to attach him permanently to the CID. The tribunal also found that two other Asian officers were discriminated against in their transfer applications to Nottinghamshire CID. In Ashford an industrial tribunal found that PC William Halliday had been unlawfully victimized by the Metropolitan Police following a racial abuse complaint. Since the Halliday case, the Metropolitan Police has installed a confidential 24-hour helpline to support officers suffering discrimination or abuse.

The Nottingham tribunal found that racist language permeated most levels of the force. A Channel 4 television dramatization revealed that such phrases as 'Come on coon, we've got work to do' and 'Nigger boy, you are getting above your station' were common parlance.[20] The Nottingham tribunal concluded:

> We consider there are no excuses – there can be no degree of acceptability. It does not matter in what context it was used. Any use displays racial prejudice. It offends minority ethnic group officers and diminishes them. There is little evidence that senior officers reprimanded anyone heard using such language.
>
> ('Race bias in the force', *Equal Opportunities Review,* 35, January/February 1991, pp. 6–7)

In 1989 the Gifford Report examined the extent of racism in Liverpool, particularly within its police force:

> We concluded from the evidence of many witnesses, black and white, that there is a wholly unacceptable level of racist language and racist behaviour by officers, including officers of rank, in the Merseyside Force.
>
> (The *Gifford Report*, July 1989, quoted in the *Independent,* 19 August 1989)

8.4.4 How people see the police

In 1989 a Scotland Yard inquiry revealed that 66 per cent of black people perceived the police to be racially prejudiced, compared to 41 per cent of white people.[21] Mass Observation Limited, who conducted the research, had already screened out of their analysis young blacks who showed 'very negative views of the police'. A third of whites, 39 per cent of Asians and 53 per cent of Afro-Caribbeans said they would never consider joining.

Young blacks' perceptions of the police have been the subject of considerable research. One of the most detailed studies, conducted in the mid-1980s by Gaskell and Smith (1985), found that 60 per cent of whites held the view that the police were 'good' or 'very good' compared to 30 per cent of blacks. By contrast, 41 per cent of blacks as against 16 per cent of whites felt the police to be 'bad' or 'very bad'. The authors' conclusion adds an interesting dimension to the range of factors that could explain these differences: it is not merely a question of unemployment, he argues, or of negative contacts with the police:

> We believe that another factor is involved – that blacks feel police hostility as a kind of group experience … What almost amounts to a 'folk history' of unpleasant, perhaps frightening, experiences with the police has worked its way into the shared experiences of black

personal experience, young blacks evoke an unpleasant stereotype about the police, and this, of course, affects any contact they have with them ... Yet at the same time, young blacks do plainly see some good points about the police. They recognise the need for policing, but object to the way it is done.

(Gaskell and Smith, 1985, pp. 261–3)

8.4.5 Black people as victims of crime

According to *The 1988 British Crime Survey,* black people of Afro-Caribbean and Asian origin tend to be more at risk from many types of crime than white people. The survey found that black people were more likely to experience burglary and car theft. Afro-Caribbeans were also more likely to be assaulted, threatened, and to suffer robbery or theft from the person. Asians, on the other hand, appeared to be particularly vulnerable to vandalism and threats. A quarter of Asians felt that many crimes against them had a racial element, as against 15 per cent of Afro-Caribbeans. The study found that while black people were no less likely than white people to report crime to the police, black people expressed lower levels of satisfaction with police response. The report concluded that, although the pattern of crime against minority ethnic groups differs when factors other than 'race' are taken into account (for example, residential and social circumstances), black people were still more likely to be victims of some crimes than white people (Mayhew *et al.*, 1989).

Notes

1   See also P. Wynn Davies, 'Colour blindness in the jury room', *Independent,* 29 June 1990.

2   According to a survey of the ethnic composition of the magistracy conducted in 1986 (see Lord Chancellor's Department, 1988). Unless otherwise specified, figures in this section relate to England and Wales only.

3   See R. Rice, 'Secret world of magistrates' selection', *Independent,* 31 March 1989.

4   S. Wallach, 'The bench that anyone can sit on', *Independent*, 12 April 1991.

5   Ole Hansen, 'Women and blacks: more chances but less promotion', *Independent,* 28 April 1989. Hansen's figures were based on a Law Society survey in 1988. See also Ole Hansen, 'A multi coloured approach to business', *Independent,* 26 October 1990.

6   See King *et al.* (1990). The study was based on a survey of 1,141 students in the penultimate year of a law degree and 1,333 successful finalists in the 1986 Law Society final examination who were seeking employment. See also King (1989) pp. 107–20.

7   Ole Hansen (see note 5). See also the *Independent,* 20 May 1991, for Bar Council initiative details.

8   *Independent,* 29 March 1991.

9   *Independent,* 13 October 1991.

10 See also Landau (1981) pp. 27–46 and Landau and Nathan (1983) pp. 186–97.

11 See Central Statistical Office (1991) Table 12.25, p. 206. In 1985 black people accounted for 12.5 per cent of the prison population of England and Wales.

12 See also *Public Eye,* BBC2, 1 March 1991.

13 See also H. Mills, 'Black people "more likely to be jailed"', *Independent,* 14 January 1991, which summarizes the findings of two local studies supporting NACRO's conclusions. One was by probation officers in West Yorkshire (see Mair, 1986). The other examined disparities in 8,000 cases in Middlesex, controlling for type of offence.

14 See also Genders and Player (1990).

15 *Independent,* 12 December 1989.

16 The Metropolitan Police Assistant Commissioner, announcing the campaign, said that extensive research had revealed that up to 2 million potential recruits were barred by their height *(Independent,* 23 January 1990).

17 *Financial Times,* 2 February 1990.

18 Letter to the *Independent,* 7 May 1990, from Wyn Jones, Assistant Commissioner, Metropolitan Police.

19 *Independent,* 21 December 1989.

20 *Dispatches,* Channel 4, October 1990.

21 See K. Hyder, 'Young blacks "would not think of joining police"', *Independent,* 20 December 1988.

9 'RACE' AND EDUCATION

9.1 'Race', education and official statistics

The issue of education and 'race' is complex and our knowledge is partial. From 1973 to 1990 successive governments did not record the ethnic origin of school children or of students in further, higher or adult education. In 1973 the Department of Education and Science (DES) pupil census that recorded the 'ethnic origin' of pupils was terminated by Margaret Thatcher, then Secretary of State for Education. Since 1973 understanding of racial inequality in education has been informed by a wide range of research conducted by Select Committees, the former Inner London Education Authority (ILEA), the Commission for Racial Equality (CRE), trade unions and independent research. The 1990s has seen ethnic monitoring introduced on a much wider scale (see Part 1).[1]

9.2 'Race' and pupil achievement

Between 1966 and 1973 the DES recorded pupils' ethnicity on the basis of the 'immigrant' status of the parents. Studies of these data, notably by researchers for ILEA and for education priority areas around Britain, showed that pupils of Asian origin performed less well than whites, and Afro-Caribbeans less well than Asians. The data also revealed that, for both groups, performance improved with length of stay and schooling in Britain (DES, 1973).

Differential outcomes in the education levels of minority ethnic group pupils, especially as measured by examination achievement, have long been a source of concern. House of Commons Select Committees in 1969, 1973, 1974 and 1977 and the Committee of Inquiry into the Education of Children from ethnic minority groups under the chair of first Anthony Rampton and then Lord Swann (DES, 1985), all pointed to the lower attainment levels of minority ethnic group children, particular Afro-Caribbeans. These reports have been complemented by local studies which reflect the complexity of definitions, claims and counter-claims involved in the 'achievement debate'. It is worth keeping Troyna's advice in mind when perusing statistical evidence on pupil achievement:

the greatest danger lies in the possibility that ill-conceived and poorly formulated studies will perpetuate the notion of black educational under-achievement as a *given* rather than as a problematic that requires sensitive and systematic interrogation.

(Troyna, 1984, p. 164)

The findings of surveys conducted in 1979 and 1982 for the Rampton/Swann Committee in five local education authorities (LEAs) with a high proportion of minority ethnic group pupils show significant inter-minority ethnic group differences. All five surveys were conducted in inner-city areas where the average educational attainment for every minority ethnic group is lower than the national average.

Children and young people from different minority ethnic groups revealed differences in educational attainment: white and Asian children and young people achieve higher results, on average, than Afro-Caribbeans (see *Figure 9.1*).

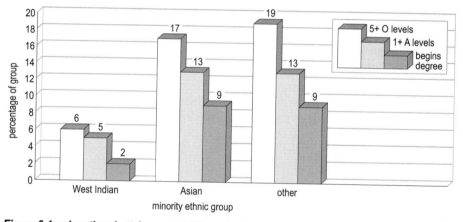

Figure 9.1: *educational attainment of different ethnic groups in Great Britain, 1981–2* *(Adapted from Statham et al., 1989)*

This picture needs to be qualified in a number of ways. First, different ethnic groups are often of very different social class composition. Since educational attainment is strongly linked to social class, some of the ostensible differences in achievement between minority ethnic groups may be reflections of class differences.

Secondly, none of these ethnic categories is monolithic. The 'Asian' group, for example, is itself made up of groups of different levels of achievement. This is illustrated by data from ILEA in *Figure 9.2* which compares the examination results of fifth-year pupils of Indian, Pakistani and Bangladeshi origin or descent.

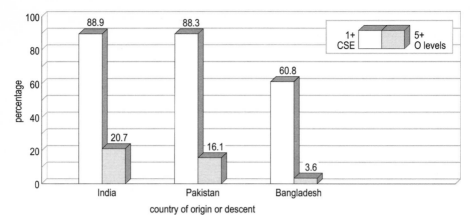

country of origin or descent

Note: '1+ CSE' means at least one CSE grade 5 or higher; '5+ O levels' means at least five O levels grade C or higher

Figure 9.2: examination results of fifth-year Asian pupils in ILEA, by country of origin or descent, 1986
(Adapted from Statham et al., 1989)

Thirdly, data collected by ILEA (which published more detailed statistics than central government or other LEAs on differences between ethnic groups) have shown Asian pupils to have distinctly higher average educational attainment than white or Afro-Caribbean pupils (ILEA, 1987).

Finally, the Rampton/Swann statistics themselves provide evidence that the educational achievements of Afro-Caribbean children and young people are increasing from year to year at a higher rate than those of other groups. *Figure 9.3* compares A-level results in 1979, when data were gathered for the Rampton Report, with those in 1982 when comparable data were collected for the Swann Report.

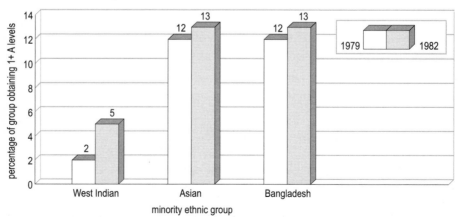

minority ethnic group

Note: There is a minor discrepancy between the 1978—9 figures for Asians as given in the Rampton Report (13%) and in the Swann Report (12%). Here we have followed Swann.

Figure 9.3: educational attainment of different minority ethnic groups in Great Britain, 1978–9 and 1981–2
(Adapted from Statham et al., 1989)

The ILEA study of minority ethnic group background and examination results was extrapolated from a pupil sample of over 17,000 in 1985 and 15,000 in 1986, providing one of the most detailed pictures so far (ILEA, 1987).[2] ILEA's findings suggest that Afro-Caribbean pupils have improved examination performance – measured in relation to CSE and O-levels – since the mid-1970s, but not to the levels reached by Asian pupils. Their findings also indicate that some Asian groups perform better in examinations than white pupils. However, ILEA emphasized that *within* the Asian category, Bangladeshi pupils scored lowest on all their measures of achievement. Moreover, the proportion of Bangladeshi pupils *not* entered for examination was higher than for all other minority ethnic groups (36 per cent in 1986), but lowest for Indian and Pakistani pupils (10 per cent for each group). The figure for white English, Scottish, Welsh and Irish (ESWI) pupils was 22 per cent.

ILEA also calculated 'performance scores' for the studied groups. In 1986 the 'performance scores' were: Bangladeshi 9.3 – the lowest group score; Caribbean 13.5; African 17.6; Pakistani 20.9; and Indian 22.0 – the highest score. The average score for Bangladeshis was significantly below the overall average of 15.2.

ILEA's data also revealed important gender differences within ethnic group performance, with girls scoring on average four points more than boys in both studied years. For example, in 1985 the average score for Bangladeshi girls, 15.1, was twice that of Bangladeshi boys, 7.6. The score for Bangladeshi girls was also four points higher than that for Caribbean boys and two points higher than ESWI boys. ILEA concluded their 1987 report by emphasizing their 'cause for concern' at the the two minority ethnic groups who performed consistently below average on most of their measures – Bangladeshi and Caribbean pupils. The ILEA report also showed that differences in expectations at intake into the secondary school were an important factor influencing outcomes. Low achievement in examination results was related to low attainment in primary school (ILEA, 1987).

A Bradford study of CSE and O-level performance in 24 secondary schools between 1983 and 1987 confirmed some of the ILEA findings, but noted a marked improvement in black (Afro-Caribbean and Asian, but mainly Asian) pupil performance compared with white. The survey found that in 1987 only 7 per cent of black pupils left school without qualifications compared with 19 per cent of white pupils. Pass grades achieved by black school-leavers were also better than those of white pupils. In 1987, 47 per cent of black pupils gained grades A to C at O-level or grade 1 at CSE compared to 39 per cent of white pupils. The Bradford researchers controlled for social class, basing their analysis on how many pupils in each studied school qualified for free meals. Using this measure they found that there was little difference among Bradford's schools in terms of black and white pupil performance.[3]

In February 1991, *The Times Educational Supplement* reported that, according to a University of London study, the introduction of the GCSE examination had failed to narrow the gap between different ethnic groups' examination results. The study analysed the results of 16,700 pupils who took their GCSEs in inner-London schools in 1988. In 1986 the School Examination and Assessment Council published criteria for the GCSE which stated that the examination should be 'as free as possible from ethnic, sex, religious, political or other forms of bias'.[4] Nuttall and Goldstein's analysis of the 1988 results showed that Indian and Pakistani pupils, who attained better results than their white classmates under the GCE system, did even better under GCSE which then gave more weight to course work in the assessment. Bangladeshi and Afro-Caribbean pupils, whose marks were below average, achieved less than ever compared to their peers. The gender gap also widened, girls gaining higher marks than boys.[5]

In the autumn of 1991 Nuttall and Goldstein released further analysis of GCSE results. The study for the Association of Metropolitan Authorities of six London boroughs' 1990 examination results looked at the examination perfomance of 5,500 pupils in relation to gender, ethnic origin and eligibility for free school meals (as a rough measure of deprivation). Pupils from India and Pakistani families fared better than those of Afro-Caribbean, English, Scottish, Welsh or Irish origin. Indian and Pakistani pupils did better in English, while those of Afro-Caribbean origin performed half a grade behind white children in mathematics.[6]

9.3 Is there a school effect?

Among the studies into pupil achievement in the 1980s, two tried to establish the effectiveness of schools. Both used statistical multi-level modelling procedures that permitted the effects of schools to be explicitly modelled in the analyses and allowed a test to be made to see whether schools were differentially effective for particular subgroups, such as minority ethnic groups. Do minority ethnic group pupils perform less well because they attend less effective schools? Do they make greater progress in some kinds of schools than in others?[7]

Smith and Tomlinson's study of eighteen comprehensive schools revealed that black pupils made more progress in some schools than in others. They concluded that 'some schools are much better than others and the ones that are good for white pupils tended to be about equally good for black pupils.' (Smith and Tomlinson, 1989, p. 305)

The sample of schools used for the research was not large enough to obtain a full mix of schools with both large and small numbers and proportions of

Afro-Caribbean and Asian pupils. Drew and Gray's follow-up work on Smith and Tomlinson's data has shown that more black pupils went to the less effective schools. However, they concluded that 'It did not make sense to talk of schools which were universally effective or ineffective; there was no single dimension of school effectiveness' (Drew and Gray, 1991, p. 168).

Nuttall and Goldstein's ILEA study on ethnic background and examination results and their study of GCSE findings also explored the existence or otherwise of a 'school effect'(Nuttall and Goldstein, 1989, pp. 769–76). In 140 secondary schools, the attainment of Afro-Caribbean pupils could differ by as much as one 'high grade' O-level pass when the full range of school differences was considered. Amongst Pakistani pupils the differences could amount to as much as two O-level passes. On the results of their study, Nuttall and Goldstein recommended that each set of examination results should carry the warning, 'These results should not be used to compare schools nor to predict their future performance.'[8]

These studies provide some support for the view that schools make some difference. But to what extent do minority ethnic group pupils attend less effective schools than their white counterparts? There has not, as yet, been a sufficiently large national empirical study of schools sensitive to the wide range of relevant variables. Drew and Gray concluded that:

> Neither of these studies relating to schools effectiveness provides convincing evidence about the school's contribution to the existence of the black–white gap in achievement … Schools certainly differ to some considerable extent in their effectiveness, but whether they are *the* major contributing factor remains unclear. To date we lack a study with a sufficient number of pupils and schools, covering a sufficient range of variables, with a nationally representative sample, combining both qualitative and quantitative forms of data gathering to answer the questions Swann posed.

(Drew and Gray, 1991, p. 171)

9.4 *Special schools, disruptive units, suspensions and expulsions*

Estimates in the early 1980s indicated Afro-Caribbeans to be five times more likely than 'non-immigrant' groups to be placed in ESN establishments (Tomlinson, 1981) and more likely than white pupils to be located in disruptive units, withdrawal classes and guidance units (Tattum, 1982, ch. 2). A CRE inquiry into school suspensions in Birmingham found that Afro-Caribbean pupils were four times more likely to suspended from schools for a given level of disruptive behaviour (CRE, 1984d). ILEA figures for 1986 to

1987 reveal that pupils from Afro-Caribbean backgrounds were heavily over-represented among those suspended from schools: 33 per cent of pupils suspended were of Afro-Caribbean origin, yet Afro-Caribbeans were only 14 per cent of the ILEA school population. The research showed that Afro-Caribbean pupils were more likely than other pupils to be suspended for a single severe offence.[9] Evidence also suggests some minority ethnic groups may be more prone to expulsion from schools than whites. Between 1986 and 1987, of 27 pupils expelled in Brent, 18 were black, 8 were listed as having 'unknown' ethnic identities, and only one was white.[10]

In July 1991 Nottingham County Council's Advisory and Inspection Service found that nearly one in four of the 449 pupils given formal warnings, suspensions or expulsions in the city's secondary schools was black. Fewer than 1,000 of Nottingham's 14,000 secondary school children are black. Their service's survey concluded that Afro-Caribbean children's body language leads teachers to think they are 'looking for trouble'. The survey also pointed to the important role played by teachers' cultural misunderstanding and ignorance in the exclusion and disciplining of Afro-Caribbean pupils.[11]

9.5 Teacher recruitment and career progression

The following are the comments of practising teachers:

I have noticed very few people from ethnic minorities who are in positions of responsibility. Amongst students there is a lot of evidence of racial discrimination – for example, verbal abuse, graffiti. It is difficult to pin down and to deal with.

I knew a coloured teacher on a temporary one year contract. She was told at her interview (initially) that senior staff were not sure that the school was ready for a black teacher – mainly because there were very few ethnic minority children in the school.

The very first day I came to the school a teacher remarked that coloured people should be lined up and shot. After that I have kept with staff who I know are not racially biased.

Ethnic minority teachers are only given jobs when they find no better teachers – all promotions go to others while we do all the donkey work and are nowhere today.

I think there is much more awareness of the needs and cultures of ethnic minorities than before. Teaching staff are aware of ethnic minorities' cultures and needs, and it is becoming a multi-cultural society.

(CRE, 1988f, pp. 54–60)[12]

In the mid-1970s the Caribbean Teachers Association estimated that only 0.15 per cent of teachers were of Caribbean origin (Select Committee on Race Relations and Immigration, 1977b). By the beginning of the 1980s, the estimated number of black teachers (of Caribbean, African and Asian origin) was less than 1,000 out of 500,000, or around 0.2 per cent. The proportion of pupils of Afro-Caribbean and Asian origin at this time was estimated to be 6 per cent (see Carr-Hill and Chadha-Boreham in Bhat *et al.*, 1988, p. 154).

In 1986 a recruitment drive for 140 primary school teachers in the London Borough of Ealing resulted in only three minority ethnic group teachers being appointed, despite the borough's commitment to an equal opportunities policy. 'Black' teachers (Afro-Caribbean and Asian) were found to be systematically denied jobs, refused promotion and confined to teaching certain subjects. The study revealed no minority ethnic group heads, one deputy head and no senior managers in the borough education department. Out of 2,400 teaching staff, only 200 were classified as 'black' and most of these were in low-scale posts (London Borough of Ealing, 1988). In the mid-1980s, 30 per cent of Ealing's population and over half of the school pupils came from Afro-Caribbean and South Asian backgrounds. One black teacher working in the multi-cultural support service told the Ealing investigating panel:

> I have often been mistaken for the cleaner or the dinner lady; anything but a teacher. You're not allowed in the staff room because they think you are a parent.

(London Borough of Ealing, 1988)

The CRE, disturbed by the high level of individual complaints from minority ethnic group teachers and general allegations about their recruitment and relative failure to progress, examined minority ethnic group teacher distribution and career development in primary and secondary education (the levels where most minority ethnic group teachers are employed). Eight local education authorities were investigated (excluding ILEA), representing a broad geographical spread, with local minority ethnic group populations ranging from 2.4 per cent in Avon to 33.5 per cent in Brent. The total number of teachers in the 1,189 schools surveyed was 20,246, of whom only 431 were of minority ethnic group origin: teachers of Caribbean, African and Asian origin accounted for barely 2 per cent of the profession (see *Tables 9.1* and *9.2*).

Table 9.1: ethnic origins of teachers in Great Britain, by sex

	Total		Male		Female	
	No.	%	No.	%	No.	%
Base: all teachers (20,246)						
Total minority ethnic group	431	*	192	100	239	100
African	58	*	20	10	38	16
Caribbean	87	*	33	17	54	23
Pakistani	29	*	17	9	12	5
Bangladeshi	2	*	-	-	2	1
Indian	212	1	103	54	109	46
Other	43	*	19	10	24	10
Total white	19,285	95	7,657	100	11,371	100
UK origin	18,513	91	7,376	96	10,885	96
European	675	3	249	3	421	4
Other	97	*	32	*	65	1
Not known	530	3	-	-	-	-

* less than 1%   (CRE, 1988f, p. 15)

Table 9.2: ethnic origins of teachers in primary and secondary schools in Great Britain

Base: all teachers in primary and secondary schools	Primary		Secondary	
	No.	%	No.	%
Base: all teachers	(8,494)	(100)	(11,383)	(100)
Total minority ethnic group	149	2	240	2
African	18	*	34	*
Caribbean	31	*	49	*
Pakistani	8	*	19	*
Bangladeshi	1	*	1	*
Indian	77	1	114	1
Other	14	*	23	*
Total white	8,096	95	10,862	95
UK origin	7,812	92	10,379	91
European	238	3	435	4
Other	46	*	48	*
Ethnic origin not given	249	3	281	3

* less than 1%   (CRE, 1988f, p. 15)

The survey also pointed to barriers to career progression for minority ethnic group teachers and confirmed career difficulties experienced by female teachers. Black teachers generally remained on the lowest rungs of the professional ladder. They were also passed over for promotion. The CRE found that 70 per cent of black male teachers were on scale 1 and 2 compared to 38 per cent of white males, while 84 per cent of black females were on scale 1 and 2 compared to 71 per cent of white females. Over half of the teachers reported experiencing racial discrimination. Two out of three white teachers thought there was racial discrimination in teaching compared to four out of five minority ethnic group teachers. Over half of the minority ethnic group teachers reported a personal experience of racial discrimination in teaching: over three-quarters felt racial discrimination had adversely affected their careers.

Minority ethnic group teachers were more likely than white teachers to be located in schools where there were high proportions of minority ethnic group pupils. Only 4 per cent of white teachers taught in schools where there were 76 per cent or more minority ethnic group pupils (see *Table 9.3*). Minority ethnic group teachers were also more likely to be employed in far higher percentages than white teachers in schools where there were pupils of their own ethnic origin.

Table 9.3: proportion of minority ethnic group pupils and teachers in schools in Great Britain

| | Teachers | | | |
| | Minority ethnic group | | White | |
	No.	%	No.	%
Base: all teachers*	(431)		(19,285)	
Minority ethnic group pupils:				
1–25%	136	32	14, 369	75
26–50%	60	14	1,676	9
51–75%	85	20	1,069	6
76% or more	106	25	754	4
None	4	1	1,293	7
Not known	40	9	124	1

* Excludes those whose ethnic origins were not given

(CRE, 1988f, p. 21)

The CRE concluded that:

> The overall picture which emerges … is that minority ethnic group teachers are few in number, that they are disproportionately on the lowest salary scales, and that they are concentrated in subjects where there is a shortage of teachers or where the special needs of ethnic minority pupils are involved. They do not enjoy the same career progression as white teachers, even when their starting scales and length of service are similar, nor do their headteachers encourage them in the same way as they do white teachers to apply for vacancies within their school. Over half of the minority ethnic group teachers believed they had personally experienced racial discrimination in teaching. There is little likelihood of a significant increase in the number of minority ethnic group teachers. In 1986 only 2.6 per cent of students in final year teacher training were of minority ethnic group origin.
>
> (CRE, 1988f, p. 65)

Minority ethnic group teachers can also face problems in redeployment. According to the Inner London Black Teachers' Group and the Inner London Teachers' Association, Afro-Caribbean and Asian teachers were twice as likely as white teachers to be moved against their wishes.[13]

9.6 Teacher training

Throughout the 1980s a series of studies examined the shortage in minority ethnic group enrolments at teacher training colleges. This is of particular concern because a higher proportion of the minority ethnic group population of Britain is in the age range from which teacher trainees come than is the case for the white majority. In England and Wales the CRE found that students of Afro-Caribbean and Asian origin made up only 1 in 40, or 2.6 per cent, of all students on PGCE, final year BEd and other degree courses leading to qualified teacher status. In the appropriate teacher-trainee recruitment age group, an estimated 5.3 per cent of the population belong to Afro-Caribbean and Asian minority groups, twice the proportion registered for courses. About one-third of the PGCE courses and a little over two-fifths of BEd courses had no minority ethnic group representation at all. Moreover, over half of the teacher-training institutions studied in 1986 had either none or only one black student teacher in preparation and only 5 per cent of such institutions had 10 or more such students (see CRE, 1988f, pp. 63–5; Searle and Stibbs, 1989).

> The absence of such role models for black children is a major contributory factor to black under-achievement. There is also the growing recognition of the value of black teachers in predominantly 'white' schools for altering negative values and attitudes held of black people and for eventually leading to a fairer and juster society ... The profession needs black teachers. The principle of equality in education cannot be achieved without an expansion of their supply.
>
> (Carlton Duncan, 'The barriers must fall', *Education Guardian,* 30 January 1990)

A 1990 study of 70 UK teacher-training institution showed that the positive perceptions of teaching that minority ethnic group students often bring with them can be systematically undermined by the training they receive. They reported experiencing direct and indirect racism within teacher-training establishments and on teaching practice: 40 per cent of minority ethnic group students reported experiencing 'racism' from initial teacher education (ITE) lecturers, 64 per cent from fellow students and 60 per cent from staff and pupils in teaching-practice schools (Siraj-Blatchford, 1990).

9.7 Higher education

According to Labour Force Survey (LFS) data published in February 1991 the proportion of minority ethnic group young people staying on in full-time education was more than double that of the white population.[14] The differences were most marked among males aged 16–24, where 33 per cent were involved in study compared with 11 per cent of whites. For females the figures were 24 per cent and 12 per cent respectively. The figures showed that all minority ethnic groups had higher proportions of students staying in full-time education than the white majority population. More white young people entered the labour force directly after the minimum school leaving age: 80 per cent of the white 16–24 age group were economically active compared to 58 per cent for minority ethnic groups.

Evidence on the distribution of minority ethnic groups in higher education – as staff or students – is, however, still relatively limited. Such evidence that does exist suggests that minority ethnic group students, along with women and students of working class origin, were significantly under-represented at degree level.

> The belief that there are too few black students in Britain's universities and polytechnics is widespread and shared by the National Union of Students and the Commission for Racial Equality. But with no proof of a shortfall and with discrimination being hard to prove ... under-representation has been a silent problem.
>
> (Vikram Dodd, 'Some are far less equal' *Education Guardian*, 30 January 1990)

A 1987 study of first degree Council for National Academic Awards graduates, excluding education degrees, showed that 6 per cent of graduates came from minority ethnic group backgrounds (CRE, 1987c).[15] In 1989 a study of ethnic differences in further and higher education courses at ILEA colleges found that black students tended to enrol on 'low-status' courses and that Asian women were particularly under-represented in further and higher education, especially on schemes involving block release or part-time day release courses (Sammons and Newbury, 1989). The Association of University Teachers (AUT) and the National Association of Teachers in Further and Higher Education (NATFHE) have argued for increased representation from minority ethnic groups on both student and staff intakes (see AUT, 1985; NATFHE, 1986).

A 1989 CRE report showed how slow higher education had been to formulate equal opportunities policies. Thirty out of 42 universities and 14 out of 26 polytechnics studied could provide no policy statement on equal opportunities. Only 5 universities and 7 polytechnics indicated that they had a policy or were operating some form of equal opportunity policy. Nearly half the universities cited their charter as sufficient evidence of a commitment to equal opportunities (Williams *et al.*, 1989).[16]

In July 1991 Oxford University announced its intention to offer easier entry for black and economically disadvantaged students. Two colleges initially joined the Oxford access scheme which was launched following staff and student concern at the lack of British-born black undergraduates at Oxford colleges.[17]

In April 1990 the Polytechnic Central Admission System published its first breakdown of the ethnic origins of applicants who live permanently in the United Kingdom (see *Table 9.4*).

Table 9.4: ethnic origins of applicants to polytechnics, 1990

Ethnic origin	Number	%
White	131,452	76.7
Black Caribbean	2,441	1.4
Black African	2,072	1.2
Other Black	653	0.4
Indian	7,146	4.2
Pakistani	3,434	2.0
Bangladeshi	501	0.3
Chinese	1,365	0.8
Other Asian	1,512	0.9
Other origin	2,097	1.2
Unknown origin	9,872	5.8

Figures refer to applications for degree courses. Overseas students (8,739) are excluded from the table. (The Times, *23 April 1990*)

Data emerging from the first ethnic monitoring of polytechnics showed these institutions were admitting fewer white students compared to applicants and greater proportions of almost all minority ethnic groups.

How students are funded could be a crucial factor influencing access. Research in Avon and Lancashire revealed that one in three aspiring black higher education students would not go to college if they had to take out a loan: another third said the introduction of a student loan system could act as a deterrent. Of all the black groups studied, Asians were most favourably disposed towards loan schemes.[18]

But the issue is not simply one of access. Evidence is beginning to emerge that Afro-Caribbean students are more likely to *drop out* of degree courses than white and Asian undergraduates. They may also receive *lower status* degrees. In the spring of 1991 the preliminary findings of a research study into the progress of 1,500 students who entered higher education without traditional qualifications was published. This revealed that more than one-quarter of Afro-Caribbeans failed to take their final examinations. The drop-out figure for Asian students was 15 per cent and for white students 17 per cent. The research, based on data from Leeds and Bradford Universities, Leeds and Manchester Polytechnics, and Bradford and Ilkley Community College, also showed disparities between groups in level of degree awarded. South Asian students were less likely than whites to get first or upper seconds, but twice as successful as Afro-Caribbeans.[19]

The findings of the first ethnic monitoring of university applicants by the University Central Council on Admissions (UCCA) was published in 1991.[20] According to UCCA's figures, black students made up just 1 per cent of the university population. (This compares with 4 per cent for polytechnics – see *Table 9.4*.) Universities admitted lower proportions of all minority ethnic groups compared to proportions of applicants, but slightly higher proportions of white students than applications received. The UCCA data also revealed that universities rejected half of all their black applicants. More black applicants applied to their local university than whites, a trend which effectively reduced their chances of gaining university acceptance. UCCA claimed that any bias caused by 'race' factors disappeared if applicants of similar examination performance were compared.

Great care must be taken with these preliminary results of monitoring. First, certain differences may be obscured. For example, black women may do better than black men; Afro-Caribbean and Asian applicants may fare differently; the locality, recruitment policies and course provision of different institutions can influence the extent of minority ethnic group demand. Polytechnics may be recruiting from catchment areas that have far higher proportions of minority ethnic groups than the 5 per cent national average – 14 per cent of the economically active population of greater London are from minority ethnic groups – while universities recruit more nationally. Polytechnics also provide more vocational courses, and courses that are attractive to minority ethnic groups, such as legal studies, are not available at all institutions. Secondly, the figures quoted often do not take into account the form of some of the findings. The minority ethnic group population in Britain is younger than the white group and comparisons with the total population figure can produce potentially misleading results. Thirdly, the quality of service is not analysed. Such data tell us little of the black experience of higher education.

9.8 'Race' and qualifications

Table 9.5 uses LFS data for 1987, 1988 and 1989 to compare the qualification levels held by people aged 16 to 64 (59 for women) for different minority ethnic groups in Great Britain. Both males and females of Pakistani and Bangladeshi origin were not as well qualified as those from other groups: women from these groups were also more likely to be economically inactive.

Table 9.5: highest qualification levels in Great Britain by ethnic origin and sex, 1987–9

	White	West Indian/ Guyanese	Indian	Pakistani/ Bangladeshi	Other*	All**
Males						
Higher	14	-	17	7	23	14
Other	56	54	50	36	54	55
None	30	41	32	56	22	30
Females						
Higher	12	16	12	-	20	13
Other	49	49	45	24	50	49
None	38	35	44	72	30	38
All persons						
Higher	13	11	15	6	22	13
Other	53	52	48	30	52	52
None	34	38	38	64	26	34

* Includes African, Arab, Chinese, other stated and mixed origin.

** Includes don't knows and those who did not state their ethnic origin

(Central Statistical Office, 1991, p. 60)

Notes

1   Our focus here is on patterns of racial inequality, but you should bear in mind that social class, gender, locality, policy formulation and implementation, levels of funding and provision, the curriculum and the management of education all have significant impacts on the educational life chances of minority ethnic groups. Only some of these can be illustrated.

2   In examining this data you should remember that the terms 'achievement' or 'performance' have been used in a restricted sense. The scores or points referred to are for tests designed for and within a white British curriculum in a structure still dominated by white personnel.

3   'The Bradford story', *The Times,* 6 October 1988.

4   F. Abrams, 'GCSE fails to eliminate inequality', *The Times Educational Supplement,* 15 February 1991.

5   D. Nuttall and H. Goldstein, 'A parents' guide of real value', *The Times Educational Supplement*, 15 February 1991.

6   *Independent*, 29 October 1991.

7   We are very grateful to Drew and Gray's review of a decade of research on 'race' and achievement in the 1980s (see 1991, pp. 159–72). For a fuller account of multi-level modelling see Goldstein (1987).

8   Nuttall and Goldstein, 'A parents' guide of real value', *The Times Educational Supplement*, 15 February 1991.

9   See *Independent*, 10 September 1988.

10 See *Voice*, 3 October 1989.

11 *Independent*, 11 July 1991.

12 Teachers in evidence to a CRE survey into eight LEAs. The overall picture varies between the eight LEAs and the information presented here is very much the general impression from all. The CRE report found evidence for good as well as bad practice.

13 Information gathered by ILEA in 1989. See *Independent*, 6 September 1989.

14 See *Independent*, 7 February 1991.

15 For an analysis of graduate access to the labour market see Brennan and McGeever (1990).

16 In January 1991 a content analysis of university prospectuses concluded that their visual multi-ethnic presence appeared to reflect a wish to attract a lucrative overseas market rather than a conscious effort to implement equal opportunity strategies by reflecting a multi-cultural Britain. See Jewson *et al.* (1991) pp. 183–99.

17 *Mail on Sunday,* 21 July 1991.

18 See *Independent*, 9 August 1990.

19 Ramindar Singh, reported in the *Guardian*, 14 January 1991.

20 *The Times Higher Educational Supplement*, 21 June 1991, reported the main findings ahead of publication of the UCCA report.

Longsight Youth Club, Manchester, 1987. Photograph by Clement Cooper.

10 'RACE' AND THE LABOUR MARKET

▼ ▼

Racism and racial discrimination accounts for most of the discrepancies in the employment statistics for black people. Generally, the over-representation of blacks on the unemployed register and in low-paid jobs still prevails, and now there is consistent research data to verify this in the private as well as public sectors ... there will no doubt be a steady growth in black businesses, but this is not going to resolve the economic crisis faced by the black community.

(Bhat *et al.*, 1988, pp. 95–7)[1]

▲ ▲

10.1 'Race' and the professions

In the mid-1980s investigations showed that while most large British employers professed to be attempting to operate equal opportunities poli-cies, positive effects were only visible among younger and more junior recruits. For example, in an investigation into the progression of black people into middle management in 1986 the *Observer* reported that British Airways, ICI, the Bank of England, British Rail, British Gas, British Telecom and Abbey Life Assurance did not keep records of black recruit-ment or career advancement. Of the companies surveyed, only the Littlewoods Group at that time monitored all stages, from job application, appointment to promotion, and they reported that black people were 'barely visible in senior management ranks'.

> Many employers still discriminate racially at interviews and blacks are often dissuaded from applying for jobs with organisations which have an overwhelmingly white image ... When it comes to recruiting for middle management jobs, word-of-mouth announcements or internal advertising can also exclude blacks.
>
> (Sue Ollerenshaw of the Commission for Racial Equality's employment promotion department)[2]

In 1988 Elizabeth Burney argued that black workers were no better off than they were before the second Race Relations Act became law in 1968. Colin

Brown drew similar conclusions in his two influential studies in the early 1980s (Brown, 1984; 1985); the first examined racial discrimination in labour recruitment, the other explored inequalities in the labour market in the context of broader life chances and opportunities. The Burney Report concluded that without positive action members of minority ethnic groups would forever fail to join mainstream economic life and that equal opportunity practices were of 'little use if there are still too few members of minority groups able to take advantage of the opportunities, because they are held down by their position in society' (Burney, 1988, p. 1).[3]

Advances have been made during the 1980s, especially in public-sector employment where councils, despite severe financial constraint, developed positive action programmes, established race relations units, improved training schemes and introduced monitoring of recruitment and employment practices. At the beginning of the 1990s a more mixed picture can be seen in the private sector, with many employers proclaiming themselves committed to equal opportunities but substantial numbers still not keeping records to monitor the progress of their efforts. In a 1990 report on minority ethnic group graduates in the job market, the Commission for Racial Equality (CRE) concluded that serious lack of opportunities in the private sector for black and Asian groups forces many Asians into self-employment and Afro-Caribbeans into the public sector (CRE, 1990g).

The civil service and the armed forces are both popular career aspirations for young people. A study of these institutions highlights the problem of career advancement and illustrates the potential impact that perceived levels of racism within an institution may have on minority ethnic group recruitment and retention.

10.1.1 The civil service

In May 1990, following a national minority ethnic group monitoring survey, the civil service announced an official racial equality programme to ensure fair treatment for minority ethnic groups in recruitment and promotion. Although there were some regional disparities, the survey revealed that minority ethnic group employment patterns in the civil service broadly matched the distribution of these groups in the general working populations, although there were significant differences in terms of gender equality. However, striking discrepancies were found in the distribution of staff above low grade categories. Variations in age and length of service could not explain why only 2.3 per cent of minority ethnic group staff were found in executive officer posts and only 1.5 per cent at principal grade and above.[4] In August 1989 a separate survey by Greville Janner, Labour MP for Leicester West, showed that black people occupied just 207 of the 18,644 posts in the top seven civil service grades.[5]

10.1.2 The armed forces

In the 1990s the number of 15–24 year olds is projected to fall by 20 per cent. However, the proportion of blacks and Asians in this age cohort is growing. They will thus form an increasingly significant part of the armed forces' recruitment pool. Recruitment data, however, show considerable under-representation for such groups. In 1988 it was revealed that only 1.6 per cent of all applicants to the armed forces came from minority ethnic groups, although at that time they accounted for 5.7 per cent of the population in the 15–24 age range (Runnymede Trust, 1989, p. 8). Within the armed forces, only 1.2 per cent were then from minority ethnic groups and these recruits faced barriers to career advancement.[6] When they rose through the ranks to become officers, they ended up with second-rate postings compared to their white contemporaries. One senior Guard non-commissioned officer told a special inquiry into racial prejudice in the army, 'There are no blacks in the Guards. There have never been and never will be. People do not want to see a black face under a bearskin. Blacks are generally persuaded to go elsewhere (P. Lashmar and A. Harris, 'The thin white line', *Observer*, 8 June 1986).

In October 1987 the Ministry of Defence had no black Youth Training Scheme (YTS) trainees out of 918 YTS trainees on its books. Two years later this figure had risen to 1 per cent (Runnymede Trust, 1988–9, p. 9). In 1988 a Defence Committee report urged that if an individual wished to join a particular regiment, his or her 'race' must be irrelevant. The report recommended the introduction of ethnic monitoring of forces recruitment, but did not recommend the monitoring of career advancement, despite finding little evidence for the beginnings of any Asian representation at officer cadet academies.[7]

The Ministry of Defence has denied accusations of widespread racial discrimination in the services. In 1990 Lord Arran, Under Secretary of State for the Armed Forces, was reported as saying, 'I firmly do believe there is not an enormous amount of discrimination in the services. I believe there is scarcely any at all (S. Barwick, 'Blacks shun forces because of race bias', *Independent*, 24 January 1990).

A report in January 1990 by Peat Marwick McLintock revealed that racially offensive views and language existed in all ranks of the services and that many members of minority ethnic groups, especially Asians, dropped out. The report – involving a study of 500 Asians, 500 Afro-Caribbeans and 500 young whites – also found that minority ethnic groups were less likely than whites to consider a career in the armed forces because they feared the forces would be racist (S. Barwick, ibid.). In a Commons written reply in response to the Peat Marwick McLintock investigation, Archie Hamilton, then the armed forces minister, commented:

The services are equal opportunity employers under the Race Relations Act, and we will continue to make clear that no form of racial discrimination will be tolerated and that all complaints will be properly investigated.

(S. Tirbutt, 'Services to take positive anti-racist line', *Guardian*, 24 January 1990)

In another comment on the report, Colonel Donald Campbell, commanding officer of the Parachute Regiment's training depot at Aldershot, observed, 'If you call someone Blackie it is not meant to be a derogatory term. It is just an expression' (A. Culf, 'Paras jump to dismiss overstated problem of prejudice', *Guardian*, 24 January 1990).

10.1.3 The Church of England

No institution is immune from racism and its effects. In October 1991 the first reported study of minority ethnic group outcomes in a religious institution revealed that racial prejudice was 'rife' in the Church of England (Sentamu, 1991). A three-year study of all England's 43 dioceses found black clergy to be under-represented at all levels of the Church of England structure. The level of racism was partly responsible, the report claimed, for the increase in all-black churches in Britain.

10.2 Evidence from the workplace

10.2.1 The use of psychological tests in recruitment and promotion

At the beginning of the 1990s concern was particularly focused on the use of standardized aptitude and psychological tests in recruitment and promotion processes. For example, in 1991 London Underground Ltd (LUL) were found to have discriminated against applicants for middle management vacancies (CRE, 1991c). Nearly one-third of LUL's 20,000 workforce were of minority ethnic group origin at the time of the CRE investigation, compared to only 3 per cent of LUL management grade staff. After the King's Cross disaster in 1988, LUL created 250 new management posts. The selection process included psychometric tests and structured interviews. Of 963 applicants, 29 per cent came from minority ethnic groups, but only 11 per cent of the minority ethnic group applicants were appointed. The CRE found that the psychometric tests particularly disadvantaged Afro-Caribbean candidates.

In the same year, British Rail (BR) changed their testing procedures for promotion following a case brought under the Race Relations Act by eight Asian guards who failed BR's aptitude tests for promotion. The tests were found to discriminate against people for whom English was a second or other language. The case attracted considerable interest from other companies, as many of the principles behind BR's aptitude tests were common across industrial recruitment and promotion procedures.[8]

10.2.2 The Ten Company Group of the West Midlands

In the mid-1980s the Rover Group decided to increase the number of trainees from minority ethnic groups after monitoring had revealed that their annual trainee intake was only 9 per cent at a time when 20 per cent of school leavers in the West Midlands were from minority ethnic groups. By 1989 Rover's intake had risen to 22 per cent. The rise was in part due to Rover's involvement with a group of ten companies committed to increasing the minority ethnic group content of their workforces. Since the Ten Company Group was formed in 1985 – members include J. Sainsbury and the Trustees Savings Bank – the average proportion of minority ethnic group recruits in the ten has risen from 4 per cent to more than 10 per cent. The Ten Company Group advertize widely in ethnic media such as *Voice* and *Caribbean Times*. They have also forged links with schools and adopted far more flexible recruitment criteria, dropping an insistence that applicants meet specified academic standards.[9]

10.2.3 Government training schemes

A series of government training schemes were created during the 1980s to broaden access and increase skills and employment opportunities. Evidence from these schemes suggests that they failed to respond to minority ethnic group needs. In 1979 the education and labour market status of all 16–17 year olds revealed that 34 per cent were in full-time education, 7 per cent were unemployed, 55 per cent were in work and 4 per cent were on Youth Opportunity Programmes (YOP). In 1988, 39 per cent were in full-time education, 9 per cent were unemployed (a fall from a peak of 15 per cent in 1985), 30 per cent were in employment and 24 per cent were on Youth Training Scheme (YTS) (Department of Employment, 1987, p. 460; see also Ball, 1989, p. 15). At its inception, one of the major hopes for YTS was that it would help to redress inequalities in the labour market, especially in relation to minority ethnic groups, and open up new areas of work for young black people. Early evidence, however, revealed significant levels of under-representation. In October 1987 the first published data on the ethnic origin of YTS trainees showed that fifty companies had no black trainees and twelve supermarket chains accounted for only 21 young black people out of

2,685 YTS trainees – less than 0.8 per cent – when in March of that year black trainees represented 3.8 per cent of all registered YTS trainees (see Gore, 1987; Runnymede Trust, 1988–9, p. 9).

In the late 1980s evidence emerged of considerable differences between the experiences on YTS for black and minority ethnic group trainees and white trainees. A YTS-leaver study in Sheffield by the Manpower Services Commission (MSC) disclosed that 29.6 per cent of black YTS trainees obtained work compared with 45.2 per cent of white trainees, and that one in three black trainees became unemployed compared to one in four white trainees (Manpower Services Commission, 1987).

In September 1989 approximately one in five trainees on YTS schemes in Greater London was black. Yet three months after leaving YTS black trainees were three to four times more likely to be in full-time education than their white peers and twice as likely to be unemployed. The average unemployment rate for YTS leavers in London was 16.3 per cent. For white young people it was 13.5 per cent: for black young people the rate ranged from 20.4 per cent for Asians to 28.6 per cent for Afro-Caribbeans (Mizen, 1990, p. 2). Young black people were also marginally more likely than young white people to leave training before completion (see *Table 10.1*).

Table 10.1: number and percentage of YTS leavers in each ethnic group who left YTS before the end of their training entitlement

	White	Afro-Caribbean	Asian	Other
Greater London	16,912	4,314	1,685	729
	67%	78%	76%	74%
Manchester	27,018	537	547	181
	73%	81%	80%	77%
Birmingham and Solihull	11,165	1,266	1,527	240
	74%	79%	82%	82%
Coventry and Warwickshire	7,327	141	413	40
	67%	71%	69%	67%

(Hansard, *1990*)

A study of YTS in London during the period July 1987 to June 1989 found that while 20 per cent of all YTS trainees in London were black, many major employers running YTS had no black trainees at all. While some employers were active equal opportunity employers, many others had less than 10 per cent of black YTS staff (Mizen, 1990, pp. 1–7).

In 1989 the Youth Employment and Training Unit (YETRU) alleged that racial discrimination was widespread on YTS. This was particularly the case among the type of prestigious employers – the high street stores, financial institutions and manufacturers – most likely to offer full-time jobs and high-quality training. These employers generally have outlets in the big cities where black communities tend to live (YETRU, 1989; de Sousa, 1989).

YTS's own figures showed that of those training on 31 December 1988, very few were from minority ethnic groups. Stores such as Safeway, Waitrose and Woolworths had no black trainees at all; the Co-op had 1 out of 158 trainees, Asda 6 out of 303, Gateway 2 out of 519, Sainsbury's 2 out of 232 (despite membership of the Ten Company Group), Lunn Poly 1 out of 564, Mothercare 1 out of 183 and Boots 4 out of 452.[10] In May 1989 a survey of the careers service in London by the Greater London Action for Racial Equality (GLARE) found that almost 60 per cent of respondents said that some employers and YTS managing agents did not take black youngsters.[11]

The situation gradually improved, largely through the efforts of a few pioneering firms (for example, the Ten Company Group – see section 10.2.2) who were among the first to take equal opportunities more seriously. Some transformed recruitment practices, advertised widely in minority ethnic group media, and increased liaison with schools and career services. Other companies began to improve their black trainee intakes. By 1989 black trainees at Dixons had increased from only 1 young person in 1987 to 5.88 per cent of their intake, Abbey National had increased from 1.6 per cent to 5.8 per cent and Marks and Spencer from 1.4 per cent to 5.4 per cent. By autumn 1989 many firms had begun to increase the number of black people on their YTS schemes. Nationally, 4 per cent of all YTS trainees were black, but still the scheme's Large Company Unit (LCU) reported that many firms recruited no young black people at all (Unemployment Unit and Youth Aid, 1990). Wide variations within sectors persisted (see *Table 10.2*).

By 29 May 1990, when YTS ended and was replaced by Youth Training (YT), black young people were still far less likely than white young people to be trained in employer-led schemes – the ones that led to jobs. In terms of gender, young women were consistently trained in lower-paid occupations compared to young men (Unemployment Unit, 1990, pp. 1–4). In 1989–90 public spending on YTS was £50 a week per trainee. Under the revised YT scheme it was scheduled to fall to £33 a week per trainee based on government spending plans released in January 1990 (HM Treasury, 1990, ch. 6, table 6.5).

Employment Training (ET) was similarly affected by cuts in funding and the recession. ET was designed for people between 18 and 59, but targetted particularly at those aged 18–24 who had been unemployed for more than six months but less than twelve months. A survey of all ET leavers between August 1989 and July 1990 showed that 40 per cent of the people who had completed their training were in work three months later. However, 55 per cent were unemployed. ET participants from minority ethnic groups were marginally less likely to obtain jobs than whites. While 38 per cent of white ET leavers had obtained work, only 30 per cent of Afro-Caribbean and 33 per cent of Asian participants had (Unemployment Unit and Youth Aid, 1991).

Table 10.2: young people in training on YTS : Large Company Unit schemes

	31 December 1988 Black	All	31 October 1989 Black	All
Financial sector				
Nationwide Anglia	3 (4%)	77	0 (0%)	152
Halifax	3 (1%)	190	4 (2%)	178
TSB	8 (3%)	272	22 (3%)	677
Lloyds Bank	14 (5%)	316	9 (4%)	256
BIBA	16 (8%)	197	6 (4%)	143
Abbey National	13 (6%)	225	11 (5%)	228
Nat West Bank	14 (7%)	193	10 (6%)	170
Barclays	31 (9%)	367	19 (7%)	285
Midland Bank	21 (1%)	224	22 (9%)	239
Sport and leisure				
Lunn Poly	3 (1%)	564	6 (1%)	790
Devere Group	0 (0%)	85	1 (2%)	67
ABTA	61 (3%)	2,491	43 (2%)	2,002
Trusthouse Forte	7 (7%)	92	6 (6%)	110
Manufacturing sector and ITBs				
F H Burgess	0 (0%)	88	0 (0%)	70
Plessey	1 (1%)	226	1 (1%)	240
Wimpey Group	1 (1%)	328	3 (1%)	321
Thorn EMI	6 (4%)	161	2 (3%)	80
BOSSF	7 (12%)	59	3 (3%)	98
Ford	17 (4%)	442	10 (3%)	351
British Gas	32 (3%)	655	36 (3%)	1,272
BMW	2 (1%)	157	10 (4%)	271
Whitbread	12 (4%)	343	12 (4%)	280
Austin Rover	28 (6%)	467	35 (7%)	526
Arlington Motor	4 (5%)	84	7 (7%)	103
IBM	25 (11%)	213	22 (12%)	184
CITB	280 (1%)	21,662	n/a n/a	n/a
EITB	7 (3%)	239	2 (1%)	271
CAPITB	150 (3%)	5,869	137 (3%)	4,455
Retail sector				
Co-op	1 (1%)	157	0 (0%)	100
Foster Menswear	2 (2%)	103	0 (0%)	115
DER	6 (4%)	137	0 (0%)	136
Gateway	2 (1%)	519	0 (0%)	440
Do it All	3 (4%)	92	1 (1%)	87
Marks & Spencer	21 (6%)	371	2 (1%)	207
Safeway	2 (1%)	227	1 (1%)	218
Tesco	6 (4%)	148	4 (1%)	465
Rumbelows	5 (1%)	370	8 (2%)	392
B&Q	11 (2%)	503	7 (2%)	474
Littlewoods	2 (1%)	147	3 (3%)	115
ASDA	6 (2%)	303	6 (3%)	230
Texas	2 (3%)	64	7 (3%)	265
Granada TV	2 (1%)	294	9 (3%)	357
Debenhams	23 (3%)	736	14 (3%)	434
Sainsburys	3 (1%)	232	12 (3%)	453
Comet	3 (2%)	144	8 (4%)	205
BHS	2 (2%)	87	3 (5%)	59
Burton	27 (3%)	802	35 (6%)	628
Hairdressing				
Steiner	2 (1%)	157	2 (1%)	142
Hairdressing TA	17 (1%)	1,468	24 (2%)	1,234
BAPHE	44 (3%)	1,486	39 (3%)	1,290
Essanelle	21 (5%)	419	13 (4%)	368
Public sector utilities and services				
CEGB	2 (1%)	526	0 (0%)	150
PSA3	3 (1%)	181	2 (1%)	235
British Nuclear Fuels	5 (1%)	440	3 (1%)	443
MOD	12 (1%)	929	8 (1%)	852
Electricity Council	28 (2%)	1,546	22 (1%)	1,576
MOD BFG	7 (1%)	415	6 (2%)	352
BR	50 (3%)	1,730	41 (2%)	1,716
Training associations				
Arrow	0 (0%)	102	0 (0%)	122
Timber Trades	0 (0%)	172	1 (1%)	224
Glass Training	1 (1%)	179	1 (1%)	186
Remploy	5 (3%)	166	2 (2%)	129
BPIF	14 (1%)	1,152	24 (2%)	1,252
Motor Agents	85 (2%)	3,974	56 (3%)	2,151
Nat. Computing	36 (7%)	499	16 (5%)	316
Sight and Sound	361 (11%)	2,772	395 (15%)	2,661
BET Public	10 (11%)	92	11 (18%)	61

Note: Black trainees as a percentage of all trainees shown in brackets
(Unemployment Unit and Youth Aid, 1990, pp. 7–9)

10.2.4 Industrial tribunal claims

In April 1990 the Department of Employment (DoE) revealed that the number of 'race discrimination' industrial claims completed in 1988–9 rose by 18 per cent, from 709 in 1987–8 to 839 in 1988–9. Applicants were successful in 54 cases compared to 61 in 1987–8, a marginal fall from 23 per cent to 22 per cent. The proportion of withdrawn or otherwise disposed of cases, without the need for tribunal decision, remained at around 60 per cent (DoE, 1990c).[12]

A 1991 Policy Studies Institute (PSI) report, sponsored by the Home Office, concluded that the 1976 Race Relations Act had largely failed to achieve its aim of reducing discrimination and promoting equality of opportunity in employment. The report found that in 'race' cases made under the 1976 Act, industrial tribunals significantly failed to provide the benefits that were originally expected. The report concluded that new laws, a radically over-hauled CRE and more public money were needed before discrimination in the workforce could be reduced (McCrudden *et al.*, 1991).

10.3 Trade unions

On 7 June 1991 Bill Morris was elected general secretary of the Transport and General Workers Union (TGWU), Britain's biggest union. He was the first black leader of a trade union in this country. The TGWU had 160,000 black and Asian members in 1991, a greater proportion than any other union.

In 1987 Bill Morris was reported as saying:

> Black people are losing faith and confidence in institutions generally, whether political parties, trade unions, the established church, or government bureaucracy, because they have failed both black people and ethnic minorities over such a long period and with such regularity. People are almost opting out of the system and searching for their own solutions.

> ('Restoring black faith in Unions', *Guardian*, 17 September 1987)

Nevertheless, government figures show that people from minority ethnic groups are still more likely than white people to belong to trade unions. In 1990 almost half of employees of black and Asian origin belonged to unions, compared to 40 per cent of the white workforce. Only a third of unions, however, had any full-time black officials. Why is this? In 1988 Gloria Mills, a black official of the National Union of Public Employees (NUPE), informed the 1988 Trades Union Congress (TUC) black workers conference:

There are many black workers who would testify their experience about how trade union structures militate against them ... sometimes it may be easier to convince management than your trade union colleagues of the need for change.

(*Independent*, 9 September 1988)

In 1988 only two of the 100 motions at the TUC conference referred to 'race' issues.

10.4 *Equal opportunities and the careers service*

The largest 'race' equality survey of careers services was conducted in 1988–9 in London. Although 41 per cent of responding careers services claimed to have a statement as well as a programme of action for achieving equality, only one of the responding careers services – that provided by the former ILEA – actually produced a written document that was considered by the researchers from GLARE to be a programme for working towards 'race' equality.

A quarter of services did not communicate their equal opportunities policies to their own employees. Over one-third did not communicate the policies to the employers they referred young people to. Less than half regularly reported 'race' equality matters to their education committee and of these 12.5 per cent did so only on an *ad hoc* basis.

Only a third of the services evaluated the effectiveness of their policies. No careers service had ever made use of Section 38 of the Race Relations Act 1976 to encourage applications from black people for posts in which they are under-represented in the careers service. Only two services had taken up Section 11 of the Local Government Act 1966 to employ specialist staff. Less than half of the services could produce figures on the ethnic make-up of their client groups. Nearly 80 per cent were unable to provide information on the ethnic origins of 1987 school leavers. The survey found only twenty Afro-Caribbean and nine Asian careers service officers in Greater London. Black staff were confined to junior administrative positions. The report concluded that the careers service of Greater London lacked appropriate strategies for dealing with racial discrimination. It made a dozen recommendations, including the adoption of a 'race' equality policy, the creation of a programme of action in collaboration with local black organisations and Community Relations Councils (CRCs), and the establishment of 'race' equality working groups comprising representatives of schools, minority ethnic group organizations, the CRC and local employees (GLARE, 1989). In 1991 a survey of 1,500 young black people by *Voice* highlighted their low opinion of the careers advice they received at school: 75 per cent thought their career guidance had been inadequate.[13]

10.5 Is there a black middle class?

Analysis of the Labour Force Survey (LFS) data for 1987, 1988 and 1989 reveals that 41 per cent of men in employment of Indian origin were found in managerial and professional occupational groupings, compared to 35 per cent for the white population. The relatively high proportion for Indian men in this occupational band is partly explained by the significantly larger proportions of people of Indian origin in self-employment. The LFS figures for this occupational band are reproduced in *Table 10.3*.

Table 10.3: employees in managerial and professional occupational groups by ethnic origin and sex, 1987–9

	Men	Women
White	35%	27%
All ethnic groups	34%	29%
West Indian/Guyanese	17%	31%
Pakistani/Bangladeshi	27%	23%
Indian	41%	Not available
All other orgins	43%	30%

(Department of Employment, 1991)

The *Voice* survey referred to above also raised questions about upwardly mobile tendencies among young black people. The majority of respondents were single people under 35 in the London area who had been born in the UK of Afro-Caribbean parents. The survey revealed a tendency for young black people to be in white collar jobs; nearly 30 per cent of respondents were qualified to degree level, while a quarter held professional or vocational qualifications. Nearly two-thirds of the men and half the women surveyed said they had suffered discrimination at work and in promotion.[14]

10.6 'Race', unemployment and employment

10.6.1 Unemployment: the national context

January 1991 saw the biggest monthly rise in unemployment since the depth of the recession in May 1981. In February 1991 manufacturing firms employed fewer than 5 million people for the first time since records began. March 1991 saw unemployment in Britain rise by 112,900 to over 2 million, the biggest monthly increase since the DoE unemployment index began in 1971.[15] In April 1991 unemployment rose by a further 84,100 – the highest official April rise since 1945. In May 1991 the DoE unemployment figure stood at 2.2 million.[16] The Unemployment Unit's (UU) index measures 'broader' unemployment levels, based on pre-1982 criteria before the DoE changed their index to a count of unemployment benefit claimants only, and taking into account some of the thirty identified changes to benefit regulations and other adjustments made since. According to the UU the *real* level of unemployment in March 1991 was nearer 3 million. Whereas the DoE data put the proportion of people unemployed in March 1991 at 7.4 per cent, the UU estimate was over 10 per cent (UU, 1991a). Using the DoE index, city forecasters estimated that unemployment would rise to an average of 2.4 million during 1992 (UU, 1991b, p. 10). In July 1991 the EC revealed that the rise in unemployment among Britain's young people was more than double that of any other EC country – a 37 per cent increase in under 25 year-olds out of work in the year to April 1991.[17]

In October 1991 the UU estimated that the number of school leavers with no job, no training place and no entitlement to benefit had more than doubled in the previous twelve months to a total of 65,000 under 18 year-olds.[18]

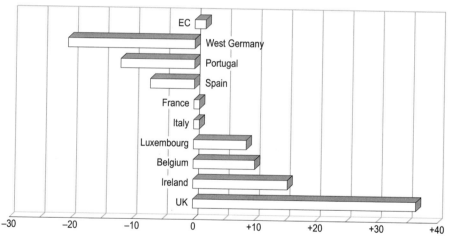

Figure 10.1: unemployment in the EC: percentage change for under 25 year-olds, April 1990 to 1991
(Guardian, 18 July 1991)

Many of the industries worst affected by the recession of the early 1990s are significant employers of minority ethnic groups – motor vehicles, textiles, footwear and clothing, metal goods manufacture, mechanical engineering and electrical and electronic engineering (UU, 1991b, p. 10). The proportion of long-term unemployed (claimants out of work for more than a year), which peaked at over 42 per cent in 1987 (DoE figures), was 29 per cent and rising in October 1990. Here, there were strong regional differences, ranging from 18.1 per cent in the non-London south east to 35.5 per cent in Scotland (UU, 1991b, p. 9). During the 1980s, youth unemployment rose by one-third.[19]

10.6.2 'Race' and unemployment

The true figure of minority ethnic group unemployment is unknown because the DoE no longer provides a breakdown by ethnic group. Instead, we have to rely on LFS to estimate regional and national trends and patterns. Evidence from the 1970s and 1980s has shown that as unemployment rises, minority ethnic group unemployment rises faster (Ohri and Faruqi, 1988, p. 69). If black people were hit hard by the recession of the early 1980s, young black people were hit harder. Black women were especially vulnerable. The recession of the early 1980s had a dramatic effect on levels of black unemployment. Between 1978 and 1983, for example, the number of black women registered as unemployed rose from 14,900 to 74,000, an increase of 397 per cent, compared with an increase of 137 per cent in the total number of women, both black and white, registered as unemployed during the same period (Ohri and Faruqi, 1988, pp. 68–74).[20]

The latest LFS analysis of unemployment available at the time of writing covers averages for the years 1987 to 1989 (see also Section 4).[21] The unemployment rate for young people from minority ethnic groups was nearly twice that for the young white population. Among the 16–24 age group, 21 per cent of the minority ethnic group population were unemployed, compared with 12 per cent of whites. The highest rates were found in the Pakistani or Bangladeshi groups (27 per cent) and the West Indian/Guyanese group (25 per cent).

Unemployment among 16 and 17 year olds rose to 90,500 in 1991, an increase of 57.4 per cent on the previous year, according to the UU. The south east of England saw the largest increase – 151 per cent. Since 1988 government employment figures have excluded those under 18 because the age group 'is "guaranteed" a job on youth training schemes'. But the UU claimed that the recession led to insufficient numbers of training scheme places. It warned of a return to the mass youth unemployment of the mid-1980s. In 1984 some 159,000 people aged 16 and 17 were out of work.[22]

According to LFS data for 1987–9, the overall unemployment rate for minority ethnic groups was 14 per cent compared to 9 per cent for whites. The highest rates were found in the Pakistani or Bangladeshi groups (25 per cent) and the West Indian group (16 per cent). The higher unemployment rates for black people across age and gender cohorts cannot be explained by differences in qualification levels. Unemployment rates were generally higher among minority ethnic groups than among whites with the same level of qualifications (DoE, 1991, Table 9, p. 68). Full details are given in *Tables 10.4* and *10.5* and *Figure 10.2*.

In August 1991 Professor Robert Moore, a sociologist from Liverpool University, was reported as saying that 'racism is wasting some of the most talented people'. Young West Indians with O-levels were three times more likely and Asians with degrees twice more likely than whites to be unemployed.[23]

Table 10.4: unemployment rates in Great Britain by sex, age and ethnic origin: average, 1987–9

	All origins*	White	Minority ethnic groups				
			All	West Indian/ Guyanese	Indian	Pakistani Bangladeshi	All other origins
All							
All aged 16–59/64	9	9	14	16	11	25	11
16-24	13	12	21	25	16	27	17
25-44	7	7	13	11	12	30	-
45-59/64	6	6	-	-	-	-	-
Males							
All aged 16–64	9	9	15	18	10	25	11
16-24	14	13	22	27	-	-	-
25-44	8	7	12	-	8	21	-
45-64	8	8	15	-	-	-	-
Females							
All aged 16–59	9	8	13	14	13	-	11
16-24	12	11	19	-	-	-	-
25-44	9	8	12	-	12	-	-
45-59	6	6	-	-	-	-	-

-    less than 10,000 in cell

*   includes 'not known'

(Department of Employment, 1991)

Table 10.5: unemployment rates in Great Britain by highest qualification level, ethnic origin, age and sex: 1987–9

Age group and level of highest qualifications held	All			Males			Females		
	All origins*	White	Minority ethnic groups	All origins*	White	Minority ethnic groups	All origins*	White	Minority ethnic groups
16–59/64									
All*	9	9	14	9	9	15	9	8	13
Higher	3	3	6	3	3	-	4	4	-
Others	8	7	14	7	7	13	8	8	15
None	14	13	19	16	15	21	11	11	15
16–24									
All*	13	12	21	14	13	22	12	11	19
Higher	5	5	-	6	6	-	-	-	-
Others	10	10	18	10	10	18	10	9	18
None	25	25	31	26	25	34	24	24	-
25–44									
All*	8	8	12	8	7	12	9	8	12
Higher	3	3	-	2	2	-	4	4	-
Others	7	7	12	6	6	11	9	8	14
None	14	13	16	16	16	17	11	11	-
45–59/64									
All*	7	7	13	8	8	15	6	6	-
Higher	3	3	-	4	3	-	2	-	-
Others	6	6	-	7	7	-	5	5	-
None	9	9	17	12	11	21	7	7	-

Higher = degree/BTEC Higher level: other = any other qualification

* includes 'not known'

- less than 10,000 in cell

(Department of Employment, 1991)

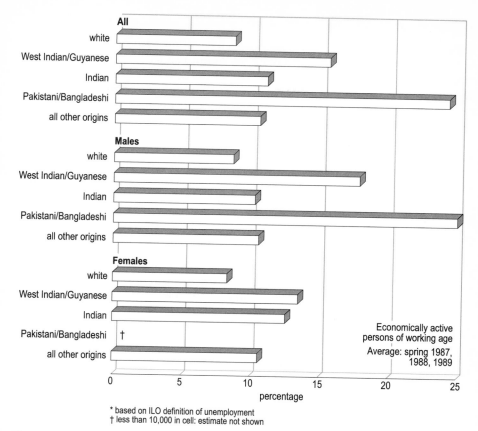

* based on ILO definition of unemployment
† less than 10,000 in cell: estimate not shown

Figure 10.2: unemployment rates* in Great Britain: percentages by ethnic origin and sex
(Department of Employment, 1991, p. 67)

10.6.3 'Race' and employment

LFS averages for 1987–9 revealed that minority ethnic groups comprised 4.7 per cent of the 1.6 million population of working age in Britain (16–64 for men, 16–59 for women). Of these, 32.1 per cent were of Indian origin, 21.4 per cent of West Indian or Guyanese origin, 18.1 per cent of Pakistani or Bangladeshi origin, and 28.3 per cent of mainly Chinese, African, Arab or mixed origin (DoE, 1991, p. 60).

White people, at 80 per cent, were more likely than people from minority ethnic groups, at 68 per cent, to be *economically active* – that is, in or looking for employment. A wide variation was found among minority ethnic groups: 80 per cent of West Indian/Guyanese were economically active compared with 51 per cent of Pakistani/Bangladeshi (DoE, 1991, Table 1, p. 61).

The data showed that for young people aged between 16 and 24 the economic activity rates for whites was 80 per cent compared with 58 per cent for all ethnic groups (the lowest rate was for Pakistani/Bangladeshi at 44 per cent). These differences are partly explained, according to the *Employment Gazette*, by the different proportions of young people aged 16–24 staying on in full-time education (33 per cent for young minority ethnic group men and 24 per cent for women, compared to 12 per cent and 11 per cent respectively for young white men and women), and partly by the different proportions of young women 'whose domestic and family activities meant that they were not available for work' (40 per cent of the Pakistani/Bangladeshi young women in this age band were in this category) (DoE, 1991, Tables 2 and 3, pp. 61–2).

People from minority ethnic groups were more likely than white people to be *self-employed* (16 per cent compared to 12 per cent), the proportion of self-employed people being especially high among men of Indian origin (27 per cent) and of Pakistani/Bangladeshi origin (23 per cent). Working *part-time* was more common among white women: 40 per cent worked part-time compared to 27 per cent of minority ethnic group women (DoE, 1991 Figure 3, p. 63).

Marked variations between minority ethnic groups and whites were found in their *industrial distribution*. For example, 29 per cent of minority ethnic group men in employment were in distribution, hotels, catering and repairs, compared with 16 per cent of white men. Minority ethnic group men were also strongly represented in health services, as were minority ethnic group women. Overall, the sectoral profile of the 375,000 women from the minority ethnic groups in employment was broadly similar to that for the employed in the white female population (DoE, 1991, Table 4, p. 64).

LFS analysis of *occupational distribution* showed little difference as a whole between minority ethnic groups and the white population: 53 per cent of each group of employees were in manual occupations and 47 per cent in non-manual. Significant variations emerged, however, between ethnic groups. Around one-third of West Indian and Pakistani/Bangladeshi men were non-manual workers, compared to over half of those of Indian or other origins. In manual occupations a converse pattern was found, with West Indian men accounting for the highest proportion – 29 per cent – working in craft occupations (DoE, 1991, Figure 4 and Table 5, pp. 64–5).

The LFS data revealed that the regional distribution of economically active members of minority ethnic groups of working age showed marked variations. Fifty-eight per cent of economically active members of the minority ethnic population lived in the south east region, including nearly two-thirds of the West Indians, more than half of the Indians, and nearly two-fifths of the Pakistani/Bangladeshis, and 31 per cent of the white population. Fifteen per cent of the economically active population of working age in Greater

Mr Bernard, Manchester, 1986. Photograph by Clement Cooper.

London and 10 per cent in the West Midlands were from minority ethnic groups, compared with 1 per cent or less in Scotland, Wales, the North, and those parts of the West Midlands, Yorkshire and Humberside and the north west outside metropolitan county areas. The figure as a whole for Great Britain was 4 per cent (DoE, 1991, Table 11, pp. 68–9).

Notes

1   Students of Open University course ED356 *'Race', Education and Society* should note that this section has strong links to Reader 3 (Braham *et al.*, 1992).

2   Quoted in G. Neale and C. Fitzsimmons, 'Wealth of talent along the slow road to equality', *Observer*, 2 November 1986.

3   See Section 5 where evidence for the relationship between 'race', poverty, and employment/unemployment is explored.

4   *Independent*, 23 May 1990 and 29 January 1989. While women occupy nearly 50 per cent of civil service posts, they occupy only 7 per cent of principal grade officer posts or above.

5   Reported in the *Independent*, 26 September 1989.

6   *Independent*, 2 September 1989.

7   See Defence Committee (1988). A form of ethnic monitoring did operate in the armed forces between 1959 and 1968 by which a quota system limited the

number of people 'not of European descent' or barred them from some regiments. The 1968 Race Relations Act led to the abolition of this practice. See Runnymede Trust (1988) p. 7.

8   *Independent*, 23 March 1991.

9   *Financial Times*, 8 November 1989.

10 K. Hyder, 'Large stores reject blacks for YTS', *Observer*, 21 May 1989.

11 *Observer*, 21 May 1989.

12 See also *Equal Opportunities Review*, May/June 1990, p. 31.

13 *Education*, 7 June 1991, p. 459.

14 *Education*, 7 June 1991, p. 459.

15 Department of Employment figures are quoted here. See *Employment Gazettes*, February to April 1991.

16 *Independent*, 17 May 1991. It is difficult to gauge the depth of the recession from the vantage point of late 1991. We do, however, know that following the recession of the early 1980s unemployment reached its peak in mid-1986. If similar conditions apply, we might expect unemployment to continue to rise during the early 1990s.

17 *Guardian*, 18 July 1991.

18 *Independent*, 28 October 1991.

19 *Breadline Britain in the 1990s*, London Weekend Television, 13 May 1991.

20 Ohri and Faruqi provide an excellent survey of 'race' and unemployment in the early 1980s. See also Clough *et al.* (1988), for an interesting case study of young black unemployment, and Brown (1985).

21 See 'Ethnic origins and the labour market', *Employment Gazette*, February 1991. See also *Equal Opportunities Review*, 36, March/April 1991, pp. 4–5. The *Employment Gazette* now publishes an annual analysis on this subject each spring (February or March issue).

22 Alex Renton, *Independent*, 13 September 1991.

23 *Independent*, 30 August 1991.

11 POSTSCRIPT:
RACIAL ATTITUDES IN BRITAIN

▼ ▼

The pervasiveness and deep rootedness of racism requires us to be continually vigilant and to understand that, simply because it no longer finds the same expression, it has not been erased.

(CRE, 1991a, p. 7)

▲ ▲

In 1984 the first British social attitudes survey described a British society that was seen by more than 90 per cent of the adult population to be racially prejudiced against its black and Asian members (Jowell *et al.*, 1984). More than one-third classified themselves as racially prejudiced: 42 per cent thought racial prejudice would be worse in five years time. Two years later, the 1986 British social attitudes report offered an equally pessimistic picture of the perceived extent of racial prejudice for the 1990s (Jowell *et al.*, 1986, pp. 149–50). In July 1991 the Runnymede Trust and National Opinion Poll (NOP) produced the findings of the largest national study of attitudes to racism conducted in Britain since the British social attitudes studies of the mid-1980s and the Policy Studies Institute's third national survey.[1]

Two out of every three white people thought Britain was a very or fairly racist society compared to four out of five Afro-Caribbeans and 56 per cent of Asians. Almost half the white respondents agreed with the proposition that 'non-white' people were treated worse than white people by the police, a similar response to the Asian sample. This compared with three-quarters of the Afro-Caribbean respondents. Two-thirds of Afro-Caribbeans believed employers discriminated in favour of white workers, compared to four out of ten from white and Asian samples. All these figures were significantly higher than those reported by the PSI in their third national survey (see Brown, 1984, chs 7 and 10). The 1991 survey disclosed that over 60 per cent of Afro-Caribbeans thought that British laws against racial discrimination were not tough enough, compared to 45 per cent of Asians and 31 per cent of whites. It concluded that confidence in black and Asian people getting fair treatment from the police and the courts had 'plummeted in the past decade'.

Most whites surveyed thought that social security offices, council housing departments and schools treated non-whites the same as or better than white people. However, while only 13 per cent and 18 per cent of whites and

Asians thought that non-whites received worse treatment in schools, the figure for Afro-Caribbeans, at 38 per cent, was much higher. One in four white people believed that social security offices gave preferential treatment to non-white people: one in five did not want a neighbour of a different 'race'.

All groups over-estimated the numbers of black or Asian people living in Britain. The true figure was around 2.6 million (see Section 1). Over half the white sample thought the true figure was 5 million: a quarter thought it was 10 million.

The survey also revealed that over one-fifth of Afro-Caribbeans said they would be fairly or very unlikely to vote 'if there were a general election tomorrow', twice as many as those from the other groups.

Finally, the survey found that racial prejudice amongst white people correlated highly with social class and age. There were also indicators that racial prejudice against Asian people was stronger than against Afro-Caribbean groups.

Notes

1 *Independent on Sunday,* 7 August 1991. NOP used a representative quota sample and conducted face-to-face interviews between 22 and 25 June 1991 across Britain. 766 'white' people aged 18 and over were interviewed at 48 sampling points. 472 Asian people and 572 Afro-Caribbean people were interviewed, each at 44 sampling points. The minority ethnic group samples were selected from the 100 constituencies with the highest concentration of people from the New Commonwealth and Pakistan. The terms 'white' and 'non-white' here are NOP's. The samples were almost evenly balanced between males and females. 38 per cent of the sample belonged to social classes ABC1 (white collar) and 62 per cent to social classes C2DE (blue collar). One-third of all the males and half of all the females were not working full-time.
The survey is reviewed in the Runnymede Trust Bulletin (1991b). A report, 'Race issues opinion survey', is available on request from the Runnymede Trust (see 'List of useful addresses').

Racism in Britain

Do you think Britain as a society is:

	Whites	Afro-Caribbeans	Asians
Very racist	10	26	6
Fairly racist	57	53	50
Fairly non-racist	26	14	28
Completely non-racist	4	3	6

Compared with ten years ago, do you think Britain today is:

	Whites	Afro-Caribbeans	Asians
Much more racist	11	9	9
A little more racist	17	10	18
About the same	28	25	20
A little less racist	33	39	28
Much less racist	6	9	8

Key:
☐ Whites ■ Afro-Caribbeans ▨ Asians
All figures are percentages

Treatment by authorities

Do you think non-whites are treated better, worse or the same as whites by:

Employers	☐	■	▨
Better	9	1	3
Worse	39	67	42
Same	44	22	44

The Police	☐	■	▨
Better	7	0	2
Worse	48	75	45
Same	36	16	40

Schools	☐	■	▨
Better	14	1	2
Worse	13	38	15
Same	61	48	74

The Courts	☐	■	▨
Better	10	1	2
Worse	24	57	19
Same	55	26	53

Discrimination laws

What do you think of the British laws against racial discrimination?

(Bar chart, scale 0, 20, 40, 60)
- Too tough
- About right
- Not tough enough

Number of non-whites

How many blacks or Asians do you think there are in Britain (population 56 million)?

Average for each group (millions)
(Bar chart, scale 0–8)
Latest official estimate: 2.6m

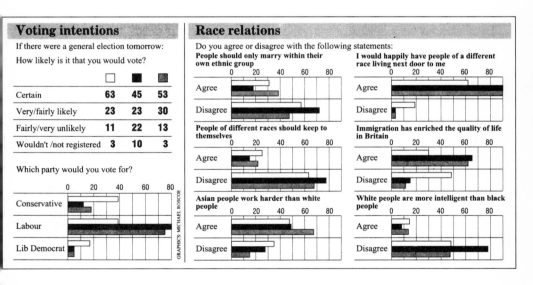

Voting intentions

If there were a general election tomorrow:

How likely is it that you would vote?

	☐	■	▨
Certain	63	45	53
Very/fairly likely	23	23	30
Fairly/very unlikely	11	22	13
Wouldn't /not registered	3	10	3

Which party would you vote for?

(Bar chart, scale 0, 20, 40, 60, 80)
- Conservative
- Labour
- Lib Democrat

Race relations

Do you agree or disagree with the following statements:

People should only marry within their own ethnic group (scale 0, 20, 40, 60, 80)
- Agree
- Disagree

People of different races should keep to themselves (scale 0, 20, 40, 60, 80)
- Agree
- Disagree

Asian people work harder than white people (scale 0, 20, 40, 60, 80)
- Agree
- Disagree

I would happily have people of a different race living next door to me (scale 0, 20, 40, 60, 80)
- Agree
- Disagree

Immigration has enriched the quality of life in Britain (scale 0, 20, 40, 60, 80)
- Agree
- Disagree

White people are more intelligent than black people (scale 0, 20, 40, 60, 80)
- Agree
- Disagree

GRAPHICS: MICHAEL ROSCOE

Figure 11.1: attitudes concerning racism in Britain
(Independent on Sunday, 7 July 1991)

REFERENCES

Action Group on Immigration and Nationality and Immigration Laws (AGIN) (n.d.) *Background Briefing on Reform of Nationality and Immigration Laws*, London, AGIN.

Adams, N. (1981) *Black Children in Care*, SS208/80–8, London Borough of Lambeth Social Services Committee.

Ahmed, W. and Sheldon, T. (1991) '"Race" and statistics', *Radical Statistics Newsletter*, June, pp. 27–33.

Alibhai, Y. (1988) 'Broken and by-passed: mental health and ethnic minorities', *New Society*, 6 May 1988.

Amin, K. and Leech, K. (1988) 'A new underclass: race and poverty in the inner city', *Poverty 70*, London, Child Poverty Action Group.

Anionwu, E. *et al.* (1981) 'Sickle cell disease in a British urban community', *British Medical Journal*, 282, pp. 282–3.

Arnold, E. (1982) 'Finding black families for black children in Britain' in Cheetham, J. (ed.) *Social Work and Ethnicity,* London, Allen and Unwin.

Atkinson, A. (1990) *DSS Report on Households Below Average Income, 1981–87,* paper for Social Services Select Committee, London, DSS.

Association of University Teachers (AUT) (1985) *Ensuring Equal Opportunities for University Staff and Students from Ethnic Minorities*, London, AUT.

Baldwin, J. and McConville, M. (1979) *Jury Trials,* Oxford, Oxford University Press.

Ball, L. (1989) 'What future for YTS?', *Unemployment Bulletin*, 30, pp. 14–16.

Barn, R. (1990) 'Black children in local authority care: admission patterns', *New Community*, **16** (2) pp. 229–47.

Bentley, S. (1982) 'A bureaucratic identity: a note on the "racialization" of data', *New Community,* **10** (2) pp. 259–68.

Bethnal Green and Stepney Trades Council (1978) *Blood on the Streets*, London, Bethnal Green and Stepney Trades Council.

Bhat, A., Carr-Hill, R. and Ohri, S. (eds) (1988) *Britain's Black Population: a new perspective*, 2nd edition, Aldershot, Gower.

Bolton, P. (1984) 'Management of compulsorily admitted patients', *International Social Psychiatry*, 30 (**1/2**) pp. 77–84.

Booth, H. (1988) 'Identifying ethnic origin' in Bhat *et al.* (eds), *Britain's Black Population: a new perspective*, 2nd edition, Aldershot, Gower.

Bradshaw, J. (1990) *Child Poverty and Deprivation in the UK*, London, National Children's Bureau/UNICEF.

Braham, P., Rattansi, A. and Skellington, R. (eds) (1992) *Racism and Antiracism: inequality, opportunities and policies*, London, Sage/Open University.

Brennan, J. and McGeever, P. (1990) *Ethnic Minorities and the Graduate Labour Market*, London, CRE.

Brent Social Services (1985) *A policy regarding transracial adoptions and foster care placements,* Document no. 24685, London, Brent Borough Council.

Brimacombe, M. (1991) 'Room to grow', *Roof*, March/April, pp. 30–2.

British Council of Churches (1990) *Return to Justice,* London, Community and Race Relations Unit, British Council of Churches.

Britton, M. (1989) 'Mortality and geography', *Population Trends 56*, Office of Population Censuses and Surveys, London, HMSO.

Brown, C. (1984) *Black and White Britain: the third PSI Survey*, Aldershot, Gower.

Brown, C. (1985) *Racial Discrimination: 17 years after the Act*, London, Policy Studies Institute.

Bryan, B., Dadzie, S. and Scafe, S. (1985) *The Heart of the Race: black women's lives in Britain*, London, Virago.

Burney, E. (1988) *Steps to Racial Equality: positive action in a negative climate*, London, Runnymede Trust.

Burns, G. (1990) 'Education, training and black offenders', *Voices,* 3, London, Forum for the Advancement of Training and Education for the Black Unemployed (FATEBU).

Carpenter L. and Brockington, I. (1980) 'A study of mental illness in Asians, West Indians and Africans living in Manchester', *British Journal of Psychiatry*, 137, pp. 201–5.

Carter, B., Harris, C. and Joshi, S. (1987) 'The 1951–55 Conservative government and the racialisation of black immigration', *Policy papers in Ethnic Relations, No. 11*, Centre for Research in Ethnic Relations, University of Warwick.

Carter, E. P. *et al.* (1990) 'Material deprivation and its association with childhood hospital admission in the East End of London', *Community Medicine*, **15** (6).

Central Council for Education and Training in Social Work (CCETSW) (1983) *Teaching Social Work for a Multi-Racial Society,* London, CCETSW.

Central Statistical Office (1990a) *Social Trends 20*, London, HMSO.

Central Statistical Office (1990b) *Annual Abstract of Statistics, 1990,* London, HMSO.

Central Statistical Office (1991) *Social Trends 21*, London, HMSO.

Chambers Community Consultants (1989) *Fear and Crime in the Inner City*, Leicester, Chambers Community Consultants.

Child Poverty Action Group (CPAG) (1987) *The Growing Divide,* London, CPAG.

CPAG (1991) *Windows of Opportunity*, London, CPAG.

Clough, E., Drew, D. and Jones, B. (1988) 'Ethnic differences in the youth labour market in Sheffield and Bradford', *New Community*, **14** (3) pp. 412–25.

Cochrane, R. (1977) 'Mental illness in immigrants to England and Wales: an analysis of mental hospital admissions, 1971', *Social Psychiatry*, 12, pp. 2–35.

Coleman, D. A. (1987) 'UK statistics on immigration: Development and Limitations', *International Migration Review*, 21, winter, pp. 1137–52.

Commission for Racial Equality (CRE) (1981) *Racial Harassment on Local Authority Estates*, London, CRE.

CRE (1983a) *CRE's Submission to the House of Commons Social Services Select Committee Inquiry into Children in Care,* London, CRE.

CRE (1983b) *Ethnic Minority Hospital Staff,* London, CRE.

CRE (1984a) *Race and Council Housing in Hackney: report of a formal investigation*, London, CRE.

CRE (1984b) *Race and Housing in Liverpool*, London, CRE.

CRE (1984c) *Racial Discrimination in a London Estate Agency*, London, CRE.

CRE (1984d) *Birmingham Local Authority and Schools – Referral and Suspension of Pupils: report of a formal investigation*, London, CRE.

CRE (1985a) *Immigration Control Procedures: report of a formal investigation*, London, CRE.

CRE (1985b) *Race and Mortgage Lending*, London, CRE.

CRE (1987a) *Living in Terror: a report on racial violence and harassment in housing*, London, CRE.

CRE (1987b) *Overseas Doctors: experiences and expectations*, London, CRE.

CRE (1987c) *Employment of Graduates from Ethnic Minorities: a research report*, London, CRE.

CRE (1988a) *Learning in Terror: a survey of racial harassment in schools and colleges*, London, CRE.

CRE (1988b) *Living in Terror: a report on racial violence and harassment in formal investigation into the London Borough of Tower Hamlets*, London, CRE.

CRE (1988c) *Homelessness and Discrimination: report of a formal investigation into the London Borough of Tower Hamlets*, London, CRE.

CRE (1988d) *Investigation into St George's Hospital Medical School*, London, CRE.

CRE (1988f) *Ethnic Minority School Teachers*, London, CRE.

CRE (1989a) *Racial Equality in Social Services Departments: a survey of equal opportunity policies,* London, CRE.

CRE (1989b) *Racial Discrimination in Liverpool City Council: report of a formal investigation into the housing department*, London, CRE.

CRE (1989c) *Positive Action and Racial Equality in Housing*, London, CRE.

CRE (1990a) *Director's Annual Report: January–December 1989*, London, CRE.

CRE (1990b) *Racial Discrimination in Property Development: report of a formal investigation into the London Borough of Southwark,* London, CRE.

CRE (1990c), *Putting Your House in Order: estate agents and equal opportunity policies*, London, CRE.

CRE (1990d) *Out of Order: report of a formal investigation into the London Borough of Southwark*, London, CRE.

CRE (1990e) *Racial Discrimination in an Oldham Estate Agency,* London, CRE.

CRE (1990f) *Sorry, It's Gone: testing for racial discrimination in the private rented housing sector*, London, CRE.

CRE (1990g) *Ethnic Minorities and the Graduate Labour Market*, London, CRE.

CRE (1991a) *Annual Report 1990*, June, London, CRE.

CRE (1991b) *Equality in Housing: code of practice for the elimination of racial discrimination and the promotion of equal opportunities*, London, CRE.

CRE (1991c) *Lines of Progress: an inquiry into selection tests and equal opportunities in London Underground*, London, CRE.

Community Relations Commission (CRC) (1977) *Evidence to the Royal Commission on the National Health Service*, London, CRC.

Cope, R. (1989) 'Compulsory detention of Afro-Caribbeans under the Mental Health Act', *New Community*, **15** (3) pp. 343–56.

Dalton, M. and Daghlian, S. (1989) *Race and Housing in Glasgow: the role of housing associations*, London, CRE.

Dame Colet House/Limehouse Fields Tenants' Associatio' and Tower Hamlets Tenants' Federation (1986) *Tenants Tackle Racism*, London, Limehouse Fields Tenants' Association and Tower Hamlets Tenants' Federation.

Darbyshire, J. (1983) 'We don't have tuberculosis in this country anymore ... do we?', *Maternal and Child Health*, **8** (5) p. 181.

Davy Smith, G., Bartly, M. and Blane, D. (1990) 'The Black Report on socio-economic inequalities in health: 10 years on', *British Medical Journal*, 301, 18–25 August.

Dean, G., Walsh, D., Downing, H. and Shelley, P. (1981) 'First admissions of native born and immigrants to psychiatric hospitals in south east England, 1976', *British Journal of Psychiatry*, 139, pp. 506–12.

Defence Committee (1988) *Ethnic Monitoring and the Armed Forces*, HC 391, London, HMSO.

Demuth, C. (1978) *'Sus': a report on the Vagrancy Act 1824,* London, Runnymede Trust.

Department of Education and Science (DES) (1965) *The Education of Immigrants* (Circular 7/65), London, DES.

DES (1973) *Education 1967–1972*, London, HMSO.

DES (1985) *Education for All: the report of the committee of inquiry into the education of children from ethnic minority groups*, Cmnd 9453, London, HMSO (The Swann Report).

DES (1989) *Ethnically-Based Statistics on School Pupils* (Circular 16/89), London.

Department of Employment (DoE) (1987) *Employment Gazette*, September, London, HMSO.

DoE (1989) *New Earnings Survey, 1988,* London, HMSO.

DoE (1990a) *New Earnings Survey, 1989*, London, HMSO.

DoE (1990b) 'Ethnic origins and the labour market', *Employment Gazette*, March, pp. 125–37, London, HMSO.

DoE (1990c) *Employment Gazette*, April, London, HMSO.

DoE (1991) 'Ethnic origins and the labour market', *Employment Gazette,* February, pp. 59–72, London, HMSO.

Department of Health and Social Security (DHSS) (1986) *Health and Personal Social Services Statistics for England*, London, HMSO.

Department of Social Security (DSS) (1988) *Low Income Families: statistics 1985,* London, DSS.

DSS (1990) *Households Below Average Income 1981–87*, London, DSS.

Devis, T. (1985) 'International migration: return migrants and re-migration flows', *Population Trends 41*, London, HMSO.

Dorn, A. and Hibbert, P. (1987) 'A comedy of errors: Section 11 funding and education' in Troyna, B. (ed.) *Racial Inequality in Education*, London, Tavistock.

Doyal, L. (1979) 'A matter of life and death: medicine, health and statistics' in Miles, J. and Evans, J. (eds) *Demystifying Social Statistics*, London, Pluto.

Doyal, L., Gee, F. and Hunt, G. (1980) *Migrant workers in the National Health Service*, Report for the Social Science Research Council by the Department of Sociology, Polytechnic of North London.

Drew, D. and Gray, J. (1991) 'The black–white gap in examination results: a statistical critique of a decade's research', *New Community*, **17** (2) pp. 159–72.

Duncan, D. (1986) 'Eliminate the negative', *Community Care,* 5 June.

European Parliament (1990) *Report drawn up on behalf of the Committee of Inquiry in Racism and Xenophobia*, European Parliament Session Document A3-195/90, 23 July 1990, Brussels, EC.

Family Policy Studies Centre (1986) *Fact Sheet 3*, December, London, Family Policy Studies Centre.

Federation of Black Housing Organisations (FBHO) (1986) *Furnace in the Pool*, newsletter, autumn, London, FBHO.

Fletcher, H. (1988) 'Black people and the probation service', *NAPO News*, August, London, National Association of Probation Officers (NAPO).

Forrest, R. and Murie, A. (1987) 'The pauperisation of council housing', *Roof,* **12** (1) p. 20.

Frances, E., David, J., Johnson, N. and Sashidharan, S. (1989) 'Black people and psychiatry in the UK', *Psychiatry Bulletin*, 13, pp. 482–5.

Frayman, H. (1991a) *Breadline Britain 1990s: the findings of the television series,* London, Domino Films/London Weekend Television.

Frayman, H. (1991b) *Breadline Britain in the 1990s,* London, Harper Collins.

Gaskell, G. and Smith, P. (1985) 'How young blacks see the police', *New Society,* 23 August 1985, pp. 261–3.

Genders, E. and Player, E. (1990) *Race Relations in Prisons*, Oxford, Clarendon Press.

Ginsburg, N. (1992) 'Racism and housing: concepts and reality', in Braham, P., Rattansi, A. and Skellington, R. (eds) *Racism and Antiracism: inequalities, opportunities and policies*, London, Sage/Open University.

Goel, K. *et al*. (1967) 'Florid and sub clinical rickets among immigrant children in Glasgow', *Lancet*, 1**,** pp. 1141–5.

Goldstein, H. (1987) *Multi-level Models in Social and Educational Research*, London, Griffin Press.

Gordon, P. (1989a) *Citizenship for Some? Race and government policy 1979–1989*, Runnymede Commentary No. 2, April, London, Runnymede Trust.

Gordon, P. (1989b) 'Hidden injuries of racism', *New Statesman and Society*, 12 May 1989, pp. 24–6.

Gordon, P. (1990) *Racial Violence and Harassment*, London, Runnymede Trust.

Gore, H. (1987) 'Two year YTS: another whitewash', *Unemployment Bulletin 23*, spring, pp. 12–13.

Grant, C. (1989) 'Behind the facade', *Roof,* **14** (2) pp. 10–11.

Greater London Action for Racial Equality (GLARE) (1989) *Life Chance: What Chance?,* London, GLARE.

Greater London Council (GLC) (1984) *A Report of the Panel of Inquiry into Racial Harassment in London*, London, GLC.

Greve and Currie (1990) *Homelessness in Britain*, London, Joseph Rowntree.

Hansard (1963), 27 November, vol. 1685, pp. 439–40.

Hansard (1965), 23 March, vol. 709, pp. 380–1, 437.

Hansard (1987), 16 November, 'Parliamentary debate on the 1987 Immigration Bill', vol. 1428, p. 785.

Hansard (1990), 10 January, col. 672–674.

Hansard (1990), 5 December, vol. 1540.

Haskey, J. (1989) 'Families and households of the ethnic minority and white populations of Great Britain', *Population Trends 57*, OPCS, London, HMSO.

Haskey, J. (1991a) 'The ethnic minority populations resident in private households: estimates by county and metropolitan district of England and Wales', *Population Trends 63*, OPCS, London, HMSO.

Haskey, J, (1991b) 'Estimated numbers and demographic characteristics of one-parent families in Great Britain', *Population Trends 65*, OPCS, London, HMSO.

Henderson, J. and Karn, V. (1984) *Race, Class and State Housing: inequality and the allocation of public housing in Britain*, Aldershot, Gower.

HM Treasury (1990) *Government Expenditure Plans 1990–91 to 1992–93*, London, HMSO.

Hicks, C. (1982) 'Racism in nursing', *Nursing Times*, 4–12 May.

Hitch, P. (1981) 'Immigration and mental health: local research and social explanations', *New Community*, **9** (2) pp. 256–62.

Hitch, P. and Clegg, P. (1980) 'Modes of referral of overseas immigrant and native-born first admissions to psychiatric hospital', *Social Scientific Medicine*, 14A, pp. 369–74.

Home Affairs Committee (1981) *Racial Disadvantage: report and minutes of evidence* (HC 424), London, HMSO.

Home Affairs Committee (1983) *Ethnic and Racial Questions in the Census: report and minutes of evidence, 2* (HC 33), London, HMSO.

Home Affairs Committee (1985) *Immigration from the Indian Sub-continent*, London, HMSO.

Home Affairs Committee (1986) *Racial Attacks and Harassment,* London, HMSO.

Home Affairs Select Committee (1989) *Racial Attacks and Harassment*, December, London, HMSO.

Home Office (1981) *Racial Attacks*, London, HMSO.

Home Office (1985) *Control of Immigration: statistics United Kingdom,* Cmnd 9863, London, HMSO.

Home Office (1991) *Control of Immigration: statistics United Kingdom*, Cmnd 1571, London, HMSO.

Ineichen, B. (1980) 'Mental illness among New Commonwealth migrants to Britain' in Boyce, A. (ed.) *Mobility and Migration*, London, Taylor Francis.

Ineichen, B. (1986) 'Compulsory admission to psychiatric hospital under the 1959 Mental Health Act: the experience of ethnic minorities', *New Community*, **13** (1) pp. 86–93.

Ineichen, B., Harrison, G. and Morgan, H. (1984) 'Psychiatric hospital admissions in Bristol', *British Journal of Psychiatry*, 145, pp. 206–11.

Inner London Education Authority (ILEA) (1987) 'Ethnic background and examination results, 1985 and 1986', *Research and Statistics Report*, London, ILEA.

Institute of Race Relations (IRR) (1991) *Deadly Silence: black deaths in custody*, London, IRR.

Jervis, M. (1986) 'Attack on structural racism', *Social Work Today,* 2 June 1986.

Jewson, N., Mason, D., Bowen, R., Mulvaney, K. and Parmar, S. (1991) 'Universities and ethnic minorities: the public face', *New Community*, **17** (2) pp. 183–200.

Johnson, M. (1987) 'Towards racial equality in health and welfare: what progress?' *New Community*, **14**(1/2) pp. 128–35

Jowell, R., Witherspoon, S. and Brook, L. (1984) *British Social Attitudes: the 1984 report*, Aldershot, Gower/Social and Community Planning Research.

Jowell, R., Witherspoon, S. and Brook, L. (1986) *British Social Attitudes: the 1986 report*, Aldershot, Gower/Social and Community Planning Research.

King, M. and Israel, G. (1989) 'The pursuit of excellence, or how solicitors maintain racial inequality', *New Community*, **16**(1) pp. 107–20.

King, M., Israel, G. and Goulbourne, A. (1990) *Ethnic Minorities and Recruitment to the Solicitors' Profession*, London, Law Society and CRE.

Kubie, L. (1971) 'Multiple fallacies in the concept of schizophrenia', *Journal of Nervous and Mental Diseases*, **153**(5) pp. 331–42.

Landau, S. (1981) 'Juveniles and the police', *British Journal of Criminology*, **21**(1) pp. 27–46.

Landau, S., Simha, F. and Nathan, G. (1983) 'Selecting delinquents for cautioning in the London Metropolitan area', *British Journal of Criminology*, **23** (2) pp. 128–49.

Leech, K. (1989) *A Question in Dispute: the debate about an 'ethnic' question in the Census*, London, Runnymede Trust.

Littlewood, R. and Cross, S. (1980) 'Ethnic minorities and psychiatric services', *Sociology of Health and Illness*, **2** (2) pp. 194–201.

Littlewood, R. and Lipsedge, M. (1982) *Aliens and Alienists: ethnic minorities and psychiatry*, Harmondsworth, Penguin.

Littlewood, R. and Lipsedge, M. (1988) 'Psychiatric illness among British Afro-Caribbeans', *British Medical Journal*, 297, p. 135.

London Borough of Ealing (1988) *Ealing's Dilemma: implementing race equality in education*, London Borough of Ealing.

London Borough of Newham (1987) *Report of a Survey of Crime and Racial Harassment in Newham*, London Borough of Newham.

McCrudden, C., Smith, D. and Brown, C. (1991) *Racial Justice at Work: enforcement of the Race Relations Act 1976 in employment*, London, Policy Studies Institute (PSI).

McDermott, K. (1990) 'We have no problem: the experience of racism in prison', *New Community*, **16**(2) pp. 213–28.

MacDonald, I. (1983) *Immigration Law and Practice in the United Kingdom*, London, Butterworth.

MacEwan, M. and Verity, M. (1989) *Ethnic Minority Experiences of Council Housing in Edinburgh*, Edinburgh, Scottish Ethnic Minorities Research Unit and the CRE.

Manpower Services Commission (MSC) (1987), *Two Year YTS: 100 per cent leaver survey, April 1986–May 1987*, Sheffield, MSC.

Mair, G. (1986) 'Ethnic minorities, probation and the magistrates courts', *British Journal of Criminology*, **26** (2) pp. 147–55.

Mayhew, P., Elliot, D. T. and Dowds, L. (1989) *The 1988 British Crime Survey*, Home Office Research Study III, London, HMSO.

Metropolitan Police (1990) *Report of the Commissioner of Police of the Metropolis 1989: we care for London*, London, Metropolitan Police.

Mizen, P. (1990) 'Race equality in London's Youth Training Schemes', *Unemployment Bulletin*, 32, spring, pp. 1–6.

Nanda, P. (1988) 'White attitudes: the rhetoric and the reality', in Bhat *et al.* (eds), *Britain's Black Population,* second edition,Aldershot, Gower.

National Association for the Care and Resettlement of Offenders (NACRO) (1988) *Some Facts and Findings about Black People in the Criminal Justice System,* London, NACRO.

NACRO (1991) *Race and Criminal Justice,* London, NACRO.

National Association of Citizen's Advice Bureau (NACAB) (1988) *Homelessness: a national survey of CAB clients,* London, NACAB.

NACAB (1991) *Barriers to Benefit: black claimants and social security,* London, NACAB.

National Association of Probation Officers (NAPO) (1988) *Racism, Representation and the Criminal Justice System,* London, NAPO.

National Association of Teachers in Further and Higher Education (NATFHE) (1986) *NATFHE against Racism,* London, NATFHE.

Nuttall, D., Goldstein, H., Prosser, R. and Rasbash, J. (1989) 'Differential school effectiveness', *International Journal of Educational Research*, 13, pp. 769–76.

Oakley, R. (1989) *Employment in Police Forces: a Survey of Equal Opportunities,* London, CRE.

Office of Population Censuses and Surveys (OPCS) (1978) *International Migration 1975,* Series MN, 2, London, HMSO.

OPCS (1979) 'Population of New Commonwealth and Pakistani ethnic origin: new projections', *Population Trends,* summer, Immigrant Statistics Unit, London, HMSO.

OPCS (1986) 'Estimating the size of the ethnic minority populations in the 1980s', *Population Trends 44,* London, HMSO.

OPCS (1991) *Population Trends 63,* London, HMSO.

Ohri, S. and Faruqi, S. (1988) 'Racism, employment and unemployment' in Bhat *et al.* (eds), *Britain's Black Population,* 2nd edition, Aldershot, Gower .

Oppenheim, C. (1990) *Poverty: the facts,* London, Child Poverty Action Group.

Parker, J. and Dugmore, K. (1976) *Colour and the Allocation of GLC Housing,* London, Greater London Council.

Phillips, D. (1986) *What Price Equality? A report on the allocation of GLC housing in Tower Hamlets,* GLC Housing Research and Policy Report, No.9, London, GLC.

Phillips, D. (1987) 'Searching for a decent home: ethnic minority progress in the post war housing market', *New Community,* **14**(1/2) pp. 105–47

Phillips, D. (1989), 'Eliminating discrimination', *Housing Review*, **38** (5) p. 141.

Phillips, R. (1986) 'No coloureds', *Roof*, November/December, pp. 13–15.

Pinto, R. (1970) 'A study of Asians in the Camberwell area', M. Phil. dissertation, unpublished, University of London.

Racial Harassment Project (1989) *Because their Skin is Black,* Sheffield City Council.

Rack, P. (1982) *Race, Culture and Mental Disorder,* London, Tavistock.

Rampton, Anthony (Chair) (1981) *West Indian Children in Our Schools: interim report of the Committee of Inquiry into the Education of Children from Ethnic Minority Groups,* Cmnd 8273, London, HMSO.

Rogers, A. and Faulkner, A. (1987) *A Place of Safety*, London, MIND.

Roys, P. (1988) 'Social services' in Bhat *et al.*, *Britain's Black Population: a new perspective,* 2nd edition, Aldershot, Gower.

Runnymede Trust (1975) *Race and Council Housing in London*, London, Runnymede Trust.

Runnymede Trust (1986) *Racial Violence and Harassment*, London, Runnymede Trust.

Runnymede Trust (1988) *Race and Immigration*, Bulletin 216, London, Runnymede Trust.

Runnymede Trust (1988–9) *Race and Immigration*, Bulletin 221, London, Runnymede Trust.

Runnymede Trust (1989) *Race and Immigration*, Bulletin 224, London, Runnymede Trust.

Runnymede Trust (1991a) *Race and Immigration*, Bulletin 248, London, Runnymede Trust

Runnymede Trust (1991b) *Race and Immigration*, Bulletin 247, London, Runnymede Trust.

Runnymede Trust and The Radical Statistics Race Group (RSRG) (1980) *Britain's Black Population*, London, Heinemann Educational Books.

Rwgellera, G. (1977) 'Psychiatric morbidity among West Africans and West Indians living in London', *Psychological Medicine*, 7, pp. 428–32.

Rwgellera, G. (1980) 'Differential use of psychiatric services by West Indians, West Africans and English in London', *British Journal of Psychiatry*, 137, pp. 428–32.

Sammons, P. and Newbury, K. (1989) *Ethnic Monitoring in Further and Higher Education*, London, ILEA Further Education Unit.

Sarre, P., Phillips, D. and Skellington, R. (1989) *Ethnic Minority Housing: Explanations and Policies,* Aldershot, Avebury.

Scarman, Lord (1981) *The Brixton Disorders, 10–12 April 1981: report of an inquiry*, Cmnd 8427, London, HMSO.

Scottish Education Department (1989) *Ethnically-Based Statistics on School Pupils* (Circular No. 8), Edinburgh, Scottish Office.

Searle P. and Stibbs, A. (1989) 'The under-representation of ethnic minority students in post-graduate teacher training', *New Community* **15** (2) pp. 253–260.

Select Committee on Race Relations and Immigration (1969) *The Problems of Coloured School Leavers*, HC 413, London, HMSO.

Select Committee on Race Relations and Immigration (1973) *Education: report and minutes of evidence*, HC 405, London, HMSO.

Select Committee on Race Relations and Immigration (1977a) *The West Indian Community*, HC 180, London, HMSO.

Select Committee on Race Relations and Immigration (1977b) *Report on Education*, 1, para 69, London, HMSO.

Sentamu, J. (1991), *Seeds of Hope*, London, Church of England.

Sexty, D. (1990) *Women Losing Out*, London, Shelter.

Shaw, C. (1988a) 'Latest estimates of ethnic minority populations, *Population Trends 51*, London, HMSO.

Shaw, C., (1988b) 'Components of growth in the ethnic minority population', *Population Trends 52*, London, HMSO.

Sim, J. (1982) 'Scarman: the police counter-attack' in *The Socialist Register 1982,* London, Merlin Press.

Single Homeless in London (SHIL) and London Housing Unit (LHU) (1989) 'Local authority policy and practice on single homelessness among black and other ethnic minority people', London, SHIL/LHU.

Siraj-Blatchford, I. (1990) 'The experience of black students in initial teacher education', Department of Education, Warwick University.

de Sousa, E. (1989) 'YTS: the racism riddle', *Unemployment Bulletin*, 29, pp. 23–4.

Smith, D. (1980) *Overseas Doctors in the NHS*, London, Heinemann/PSI.

Smith, D. and Tomlinson, S. (1989) *The School Effect: a study of multi-racial comprehensives*, London, Policy Studies Group.

Smith, S. (1989) *The Politics of 'Race' and Residence,* Oxford, Polity Press.

Smith, S. and Hill, S. (1991) 'Unwelcome home', *Roof,* **16** (2) pp. 38–41.

Social Security Committee (1991) *Low Income Statistics: households below average income, 1988,* first report, London, HMSO.

Statham, J., Donald, M. and Cathcart, H. (1989) *The Education Factfile,* Sevenoaks, Hodder and Staughton.

Statistical Monitoring Unit (1991) *Meaningful Statistics on Poverty,* Statistical Monitoring Unit, University of Bristol.

Tattum, D. P. (1982) *Disruptive Pupils in Schools and Units*, Chichester, John Wiley.

Thomas, M. and Williams, S. (1972) 'Overseas nurses in Britain: a PEP study for the UK Council for Overseas Student Affairs', *Broadsheet 539*, London, Political and Economic Planning.

Tomlinson, S. (1981) *Educational Subnormality: a study in decision making,* London, Routledge and Kegan Paul.

Torkington, N. (1983) *The Racial Politics of Health: A Liverpool profile*, Merseyside Area Profile Group, University of Liverpool.

Townsend, P. (1991) *The Poor are Poorer,* Statistical Monitoring Unit, University of Bristol.

Townsend, P. and Davidson, N. (eds) (1982) *Inequalities in Health* (The Black Report), Harmondsworth, Penguin.

Troyna, B. (1984) 'Fact or artefact? The "educational under achievement" of black pupils', *British Journal of Sociology of Education*, **5** (2) pp. 153–60.

Troyna, B. and Hatcher, R. (1992) 'Racial incidents in schools: a framework for analysis and intervention', in Gill *et al.* (eds), *Racism and Education: structures and strategies,* London, Sage/Open University.

Tuck, S. (1982) 'Sickle cell disease and pregnancy', *British Journal of Hospital Medicine*, August, pp. 123–7.

Unemployment Unit (1990) 'YT: graduating from YTS', *Unemployment Bulletin,* 33, summer.

Unemployment Unit and Youth Aid (1990) *Unemployment Bulletin*, 32, spring.

Unemployment Unit and Youth Aid (1991) *ET Leavers Survey.*

Victim Support (1991) *Racial Attacks in Camden, Southwark and Newham,* London, Victim Support.

Vincent, J. (1985) *The State of the Nation*, London, Pan.

West Midlands County Council (1986) *A Different Reality: report of the Review Panel into the Handsworth Rebellions of 1985*, West Midland County Council.

West Midlands Low Pay Unit (1988) *Last Among Equals*, Birmingham, West Midlands Low Pay Unit.

Westwood, S. *et al.* (1989) *Sadness in My Heart: racism and mental health – a research report*, Leicester, Leicester Black Mental Health Group.

White, R. M. (1979) 'What's in a name? problems in official and legal usages of race', *New Community*, **7** (3) pp. 333–47.

Whitehead, M. (1987) *The Health Divide*, London, Health Education Council.

Wilkinson, A. (1982) *Children who come into care in Tower Hamlets,* Directorate of Social Services, London Borough of Tower Hamlets.

Williams, J., Cocking, J. and Davies, L. (1989) *Words or Deeds*, London, CRE.

Youth Employment and Training Unit (YETRU) (1989) *The Firms That Like to Say 'No'!*, London, YETRU.

Acronyms and abbreviations

BCC	British Council of Churches
CCETSW	Central Council for Education and Training in Social Work
CPAG	Child Poverty Action Group
CRC	Community Relations Council
CRE	Commission for Racial Equality
ESWI	English, Scottish, Welsh and Irish
FATEBU	Forum for the Advancement of Training and Education for the Black Unemployed
FBHO	Federation of Black Housing Organizations
GLARE	Greater London Action for Racial Equality
GLC	Greater London Council (abolished in 1986)
ILEA	Inner London Education Authority (abolished in 1990)
IRR	Institute of Race Relations
LFS	Labour Force Survey
LEA	Local Education Authority
MORI	Market and Opinion Research Institute
NACAB	National Association of Citizens' Advice Bureaux
NACRO	National Association for the Care and Resettlement of Offenders
NAPO	National Association of Probation Officers
NCWP	New Commonwealth and Pakistan (the New Commonwealth includes all Commonwealth countries except Australia, Canada and New Zealand)

OPCS	Office of Population Censuses and Surveys
PRT	Prison Reform Trust
PSI	Policy Studies Institute
RSRG	Radical Statistics Race Group
UNICEF	United Nations International Children's Emergency Fund
UU	Unemployment Unit
YETRU	Youth Employment and Training Unit

List of useful addresses

Black Mental Health Group
The Playtower
Ladywell Road
London SE13 7UW

Board of Deputies of British Jews
Woburn House (4th floor)
Upper Woburn Place
London WC1H OEP

Campaign for Anti Racist
Education (CARE)
PO Box 681
London SW8 1SX

Centre for Multicultural Education
University of London Institute of
Education
20 Bedford Way
London WC1H 0AL

Centre for Research in Ethnic
Relations
University of Warwick
Coventry CV4 7AL

Centre for the Study of Islam and
Christian Muslim Relations
Selly Oak College
Birmingham B29 6LE

Child Poverty Action Group
1–5 Bath Street
London W1V 3DG

Commission for Racial Equality
(Head Office)
Elliot House
10–12 Allington Street
London SW1E 5EH

Commission of the European
Communities
Directorate-General Information
Rue de la Loi
B–1049
Brussels

Citizen's Advice Bureau (Scotland)
26 George Square
Edinburgh EH8 9LD

Commonwealth Institute
Kensington High Street
London W8 6NQ

Community and Race Relations
Unit
British Council of Churches
Inter-Church House
35–41 Lower Marsh
London SE1 7RL

Equal Opportunities Commission
Quay Street
Manchester M3 3HN

Equal Rights Department
TUC
Congress House
London WC1B 3LS

Ethnic Minorities Development
Unit
35 Vine Street
Hillfields
Coventry CV1 5HN

Family Policy Studies Centre
231 Baker Street
London NW1 6XE

Greater London Action for Racial
Equality (formerly LACRC)
St Margaret's House
21 Old Ford Road
London E2 9PL

Home Office:
Immigration and Nationality
Department
Lunar House
Wellesley Road
Croydon CR9 2BY

Institute of Race Relations
2–6 Leeke Street
London WC1X 9HS

Joint Council for the Welfare of
Immigrants
115 Old Street
London EC1V 9JR

Minority Rights Group
29 Craven Street
London WC2N 5NG

Liberty
(formerly National Council for Civil
Liberties)
21 Tabard Street
London SE1 4LA

NACRO
169 Clapham Road
London SW9 0PU

National Association of Citizens
Advice Bureaux
115 Pentonville Road
London N1 9LZ

National Antiracist Movement in
Education (NAME)
41 Strawberry Lane
Carshalton
Surrey SM5 2NG

National Association of Racial
Equality Councils
8–10 Coroner Street (1st floor)
London N1 6HD

National Council for Voluntary
Organisations
26 Beford Square
London SE13 7UW

Newham Monitoring Project
382 Katherine Road
London E7 8NW

Office of Populations Censuses and
Surveys
Census Division
Room 823
St Catherines House
10 Kingsway
London WC2B 6JP

Runnymede Trust
11 Princelet Street
London E1 6QH

The Unemployment Unit
9 Poland Street
London W1V 3DG

Acknowledgements

Grateful acknowledgment is made to the following sources for permission to reproduce material in this book:

Cover photograph
From *Presence*, 1988, Manchester © Cornerhouse Publications and Clement Cooper; Longsight Youth Club, page 131, also from *Presence* © Cornerhouse Publications and Clement Cooper; Mr Bernard, page 149, © Clement Cooper.

Text
p. 100: Pilger, J. (1987) 'Nasreen, voice of outrage from a house under siege', *Independent*, 2 February 1987.

Figures
Figure 1.1: Fothergill, S. and Vincent, J. (1985) in Kidron, M., *The State of the Nation*, Pluto Press Ltd, copyright © Pluto Press Ltd; *Figures 1.2, 1.3, 1.4, & 1.5:* Office of Population Censuses and Surveys, Labour Force Survey Reports, 1981, 1986–8, adapted with the permission of the Controller of Her Majesty's Stationery Office; *Figures 1.6, 1.7 & 2.1:* Central Statistical Office / OPCS (1990) *Social Trends 20,* adapted with the permission of the Controller of Her Majesty's Stationery Office; *Figure 1.8:* Office of Population Censuses and Surveys, Labour Force Survey Reports, 1985–7, adapted with the permission of the Controller of Her Majesty's Stationery Office; *Figures 1.9 & 1.10:* Haskey, J. (1989) 'Families and households of the ethnic minority and white populations of Great Britain', *Population Trends 57*, Office of Population Censuses and Surveys, adapted with the permission of the Controller of Her Majesty's Stationery Office; *Figure 2.1:* Central Statistical Office / OPCS (1990) *Social Trends 20*, adapted with the permission of the Controller of Her Majesty's Stationery Office; *Figure 2.2:* published by permission of *The Guardian*; *Figure 3.1:* The Independent, 13 February 1991; *Figure 3.2:* John Sturrock, Network; *Figure 3.3:* Denis Doran, Network; *Figure 4.1:* Frayman, H. (1990) *Breadline Britain 1990s*, Domino Films / London Weekend Television; *Figures 4.2 & 4.3: The Independent*, 29 July 1990; *Figures 4.4, 4.5 & 4.6:* Oppenheim, C. (1990) *Poverty – the Facts,* Child Poverty Action Group; *Figures 4.7 & 4.8:* Ormerod, P. and Salama, E. (1990) 'The rise of the British underclass', *The Independent*, 19 June 1990; *Figure 5.1:* Britton M. (1989) 'Mortality and geography' in *Population Trends 56*, summer, Office of Population Censuses and Surveys, adapted with the permission of the Controller of Her Majesty's Stationery Office; *Figure 7.1:* David Hoffmann; *Figure 10.1:* reproduced by permission of *The Guardian*; *Figure 10.2:* Department of Employment (1991) *Employment Gazette*, February, adapted with the

permission of the Controller of Her Majesty's Stationery Office; *Figure 11.1:*
Cohen, N. (1991) 'Racism: someone else is to blame', *Independent on
Sunday,* 7 July 1991.

Tables

Table 1.1: Office of Population Censuses and Surveys, *Labour Force Survey
Reports,* 1981, 1986–8, adapted with the permission of the Controller of Her
Majesty's Stationery Office; *Table 1.2:* Haskey, J. (1991) *Population Trends
63*, spring, Office of Population Censuses and Surveys, adapted with the
permission of the Controller of Her Majesty's Stationery Office; *Table 2.1:*
Central Statistical Office (1990) *Annual Abstract of Statistics,* adapted with
the permission of the Controller of Her Majesty's Stationery Office; *Tables
4.1 & 6.2:* Brown, C. (1984) *Black and White Britain,* Gower; *Table 6.1:*
Barn, R. (1990) 'Black children in local authority care: admission patterns',
New Community, 16 (2) January, Commission for Racial Equality; *Tables
7.1 & 9.5:* Central Statistical Office / OPCS (1991) *Social Trends 21*,
adapted with the permission of the Controller of Her Majesty's Stationery
Office; *Table 8.1:* courtesy of the Law Society; *Table 8.2:* McDermott, K.
(1990) 'We have no problem: the experience of racism in prison', *New
Community,* 16 (2) January, Commission for Racial Equality; *Table 8.3:*
reproduced by kind permission of *Today* newspaper; *Tables 9.1, 9.2, 9.3:*
CRE (1988), *Ethnic Minority School Teachers*, Commission for Racial
Equality; *Table 9.4: The Times,* 23 April 1990, courtesy of the Polytechnics
Central Admission System; *Table 10.1: Hansard,* 10 January 1990,
Parliamentary Copyright; *Table 10.2:* Unemployment Unit (1990)
Unemployment Bulletin, 32, spring; *Tables 10.3, 10.4 & 10.5:* Department of
Employment (1991) *Employment Gazette*, February, adapted with the
permission of the Controller of Her Majesty's Stationery Office.

Maps

Maps 1.1, 1.2, 1.3, 1.4, & 1.5: Haskey, J. (1991) 'The ethnic minority
populations resident in private households: estimates by county and
metropolitan district of England and Wales', *Population Trends 63*, Office of
Population Censuses and Surveys, reproduced with the permission of the
Controller of Her Majesty's Stationery Office.